The BEGINNER'S

GOSPEL

STORY BIBLE

Jared Kennedy

Illustrated by Trish Mahoney

New Growth Press, Greensboro, NC 27404
Text Copyright © 2017 by Jared Kennedy
Illustration Copyright © 2017 by Trish Mahoney

Art and Design: Trish Mahoney

ISBN: 978-1-945270-04-8 (Print)
ISBN: 978-1-945270-81-9 (eBook)

Library of Congress Cataloging-in-Publication Data
Names: Kennedy, Jared, 1978- author.
Title: The beginner's gospel story Bible / Jared Kennedy.
Description: Greensboro, NC : New Growth Press, 2017.
Identifiers: LCCN 2017012767 | ISBN 9781945270048 (trade cloth)
Subjects: LCSH: Bible stories, English.
Classification: LCC BS551.3 .K44 2017 | DDC 225.9/505--dc23
LC record available at https://lccn.loc.gov/2017012767

Printed in China

28 27 26 25 24 23 22 21   4 5 6 7 8

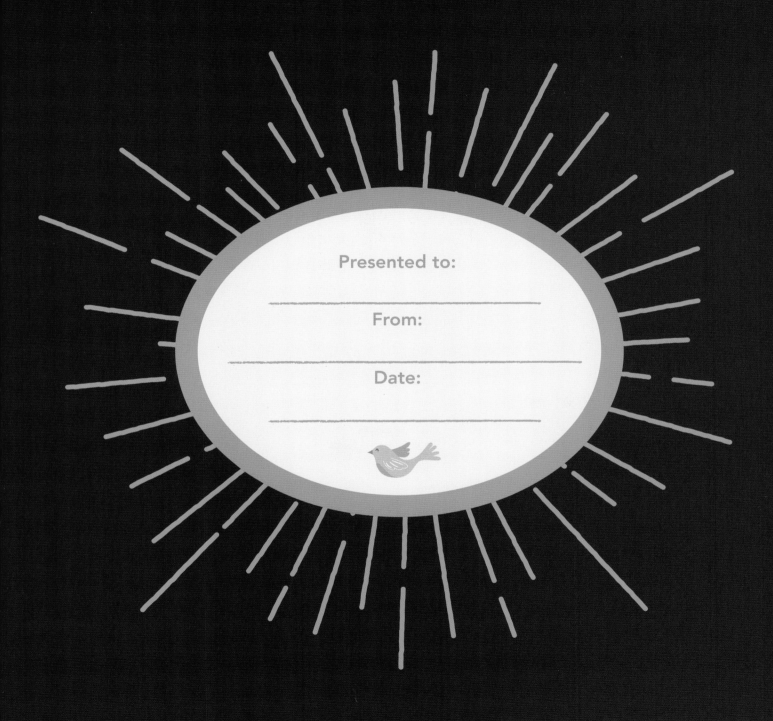

Presented to:

_____

From:

_____

Date:

_____

Contents

Old Testament: Promises Made

New Testament: Promises Kept

Introduction

Kids know the value of a promise. A parent's commitment to go out for ice cream inspires hope. Disappointment reigns when the shop closes early. Broken promises can bring tears. Unlike human parents, our good and all-powerful God always keeps his word (Numbers 23:19). And the way he fulfills his promises is better than anyone could have imagined!

The Beginner's Gospel Story Bible traces God's perfect promises through the stories of the Old and New Testament. In every story, one key truth to remember is highlighted in bold letters. Each story also ends with a question you can use to further reinforce this truth with your child. Colorful illustrations add fun teaching elements of counting, opposites, patterns, and object recognition. Read a chapter at a time with your child. Let your early-reader read to you. If you have older kids, look up and read the Bible passages listed after each story title. Since there are 52 stories, you also may consider teaching one per week as part of a yearlong Bible curriculum. I pray even our youngest kids will come to know that God's promises are especially for them and that all of his promises are "Yes" and "Amen" in Jesus.

OLD
TESTAMENT

PROMISES MADE

Once there was no sky, no trees, and no animals.
The world was empty like a blank piece of paper.

Then

God made everything.

God didn't use crayons or stickers like we do when we
make things. God used only words. He said, "Let there be
sky and water, land and plants, sun and moon."

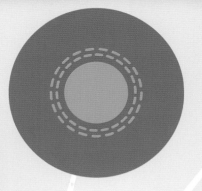

Then . . .

POP!

There they were.

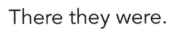

God made trees and hills for climbing. He made lakes and oceans for swimming. He made nuts and raspberries and apples and everything good to eat.

Then God made all of the animals. Birds to fly in the clouds. Fish to swim in the water. Goats to climb on the mountains. Monkeys to swing in the trees.

God looked at what he had made and he said,

"This is good."

God wasn't done. He saved his most special creation for last.
Do you know what was missing? Us.
There were no mommies and daddies. No sisters and brothers.
No friends.

Do you know how
many people God
started with?
Just 2.

1
man

His name was Adam.

1
woman

Her name was Eve.

God made Adam and Eve
to be like him.

What is your favorite thing God has made?

God made everything.
He was happy with the world
he made. He wants you to
enjoy it too.

God gave Adam and Eve a big garden filled
with trees that had delicious fruit. God showed
Adam and Eve that he loved them very much.
He gave them one rule to obey so they could
show God they loved him too.

"You can eat fruit from any of the trees in the garden except **THIS** one," said God.

"If you eat fruit from **THIS** tree, you will die."

Now God has an enemy. His name is Satan.
Satan came into the garden looking like a tricky snake.
He lied to Adam and Eve.

"God's rules
are silly,"
Satan said.

"You won't die if you eat this fruit. You will
be wise and happy like God."

Adam and Eve forgot
that God loved them.
Eve listened to Satan.

The fruit looked yummy, so she
ate some. She gave it to Adam
who ate some too.

Oh no!

Adam and Eve disobeyed God.

Before, they were glad to see God and talk with him, but now they were afraid of God.

It was sad.

God said, "Life will be hard, and one day you will die."

Because they disobeyed, they could not live with God in the garden anymore.

But God still loved Adam and Eve. He made a promise they would live with him again. God said, "I will send you a Savior. He will fight against my enemy Satan. The Savior will bring you back to me."

Can you think of a time you disobeyed?

We all disobey God, but Jesus still loves us. Jesus is the Savior God promised. Jesus fights against all evil and sin.

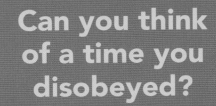

When we disobey, Jesus brings us back to God.

13

Adam and Eve had children, and their children had children.

Instead of doing what God said was right, all those children did what they wanted all the time.

Now the whole world **was in trouble.**

God was sad because of all the bad choices people were making. God said, "I will cover the world with water. I'll start over with one family."

God chose Noah and his family.

God said to Noah,

"Build a gigantic boat—an ark,"

and Noah obeyed.

God told Noah to put two of each kind of animal in the ark.

So in went lions and lizards, beavers and bears, dogs and donkeys, and all kinds of other animals too! Then God told Noah's family to get inside the ark. At last God shut the door.

The rains came. A flood came.

It rained forty days and nights.

Water was everywhere.

But God didn't forget about Noah, his family, and the animals. God remembered. He kept Noah safe in the ark.

Finally God made the rain stop.
All the water drained away.

Sssluuuurrrrrp.

The flood was gone.
God made a promise to Noah:
"I will never flood the
whole world again."
Hooray!

God **always** keeps his promises.

Look at the sky.
What do you see?
It's a rainbow.
God put a rainbow
in the sky to help
Noah remember
God's promise.

purple blue green yellow orange red

Can you remember some of God's promises?

God promised to keep his children safe with Jesus
just like Noah and his family were safe in the ark.

STORY 4
Abraham
Counts the Stars

Genesis 12:1–9;
15:1–21
Psalm 147:4

Do you remember how God promised Adam and Eve he would send a Savior? God picked Abraham to be part of that big plan.

God said to Abraham, "Leave your home. Leave your friends. Go to a new land. Go to the new home I'm giving to you."

Abraham loved God. So he obeyed. He left his home and his friends.
God made Abraham the first member of his special family.
Then God gave Abraham and his wife Sarah:

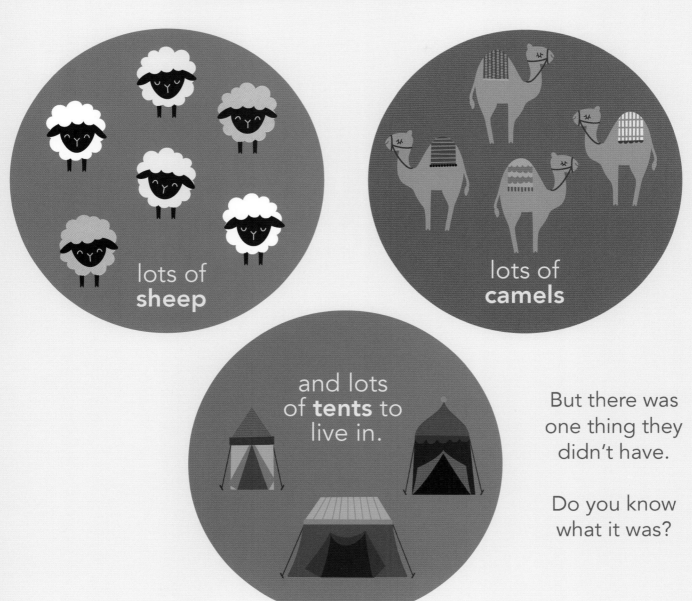

lots of
sheep

lots of
camels

and lots
of **tents** to
live in.

But there was
one thing they
didn't have.

Do you know
what it was?

They didn't have any children. Not
even one. Abraham was sad.
"Did God forget us?"
Abraham wondered. No.

God never
forgets his people.

God said, "Abraham, look up at the sky. Count the stars."
Abraham looked up, but he couldn't count the stars.
There were way too many!
"I have not forgotten you," said God.
Then God made a promise, "I will give you a baby boy. Your family
will have as many people in it as there are stars in the sky."

Can you count all
the stars in the picture?

The stars help us remember
that God kept his promise to
Abraham. God will never leave
his people. He always
remembers his children just like
he remembered Abraham.

23

Abraham and Sarah waited a long, long, long time. But one day they had a baby boy named Isaac. His name means "laughter."

Abraham and Sarah were so happy that they laughed!

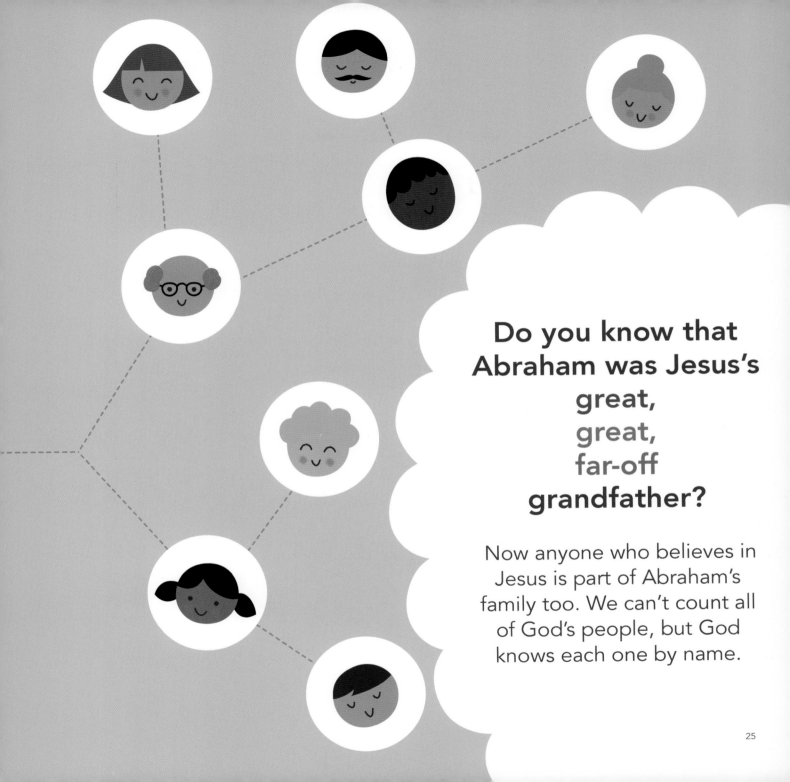

Do you know that Abraham was Jesus's great, great, far-off grandfather?

Now anyone who believes in Jesus is part of Abraham's family too. We can't count all of God's people, but God knows each one by name.

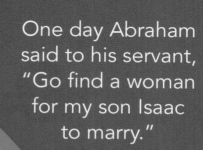

Isaac grew up.

One day Abraham
said to his servant,
"Go find a woman
for my son Isaac
to marry."

The servant was worried, and he said,
"What if I can't find a wife for Isaac?"
"Don't be afraid," answered Abraham.

"God will help us.

He will keep his promise."

The servant obeyed. He loaded his camels with gifts,
and he traveled a long way across a dry, dusty desert.

Finally the servant came to a well. He stopped and prayed,
"God, please show me just the right woman for Isaac.

I will know she is the one if she says,
'I will get water for you. . . AND I will get water
for your thirsty camels too.'"

While the servant was praying, a beautiful woman named Rebekah
came to the well. "Can I get you some water?" she asked.

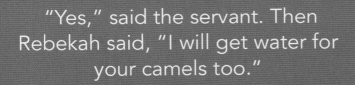

"Yes," said the servant. Then Rebekah said, "I will get water for your camels too."

Have you ever asked God to help you?

God helped Abraham's servant find Rebekah. Rebekah married Isaac, and many, many years later, Jesus was born into their family. Do you need God's help today? You can ask God for help right now.

STORY 6
Surprise! God
Chooses Jacob

Genesis 25:19–34
Romans 9:10–13
1 Corinthians 1:26–30

Isaac and Rebekah got married. Then God spoke to Rebekah in a dream.

Big

Little

God promised, "You will have two baby boys—twins. And here is another surprise—the **BIG** brother will serve the **LITTLE** brother." Before the boys were born, God chose the little brother.

The dream came true. Isaac and Rebekah had two boys. Jacob was the little brother. He liked to stay inside to help his mother cook.

Esau was bigger and stronger than Jacob. He liked to hunt for food outside with his father.

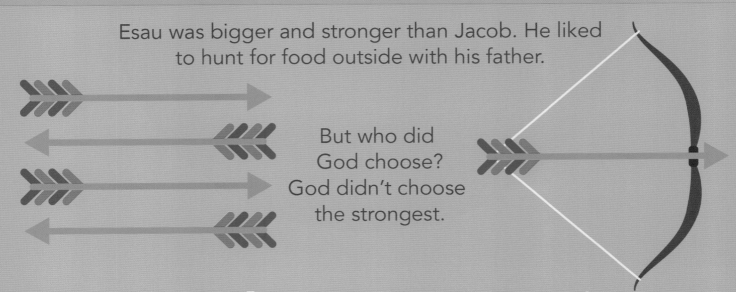

But who did God choose? God didn't choose the strongest.

God's choice is a surprise.

Before the boys were born, God chose Jacob.

One day Jacob cooked some **delicious red stew.**

Esau was tired and hungry. Esau said, "Jacob, give me some of that stew." Jacob didn't share right away. **Jacob was jealous and tricky.**

Jacob said to Esau, "I will give it to you if you let me take your place and be the big brother." That wasn't a kind thing to say. But God didn't choose the nicest brother. God chose Jacob.

Did you know?

God doesn't choose the strongest or the best. God chooses people who need him. He chooses weak and sinful people like Jacob, and you, and me. Thank you, God, for your surprising choice.

Esau said, "I'm so hungry. You can be the big brother." Esau sold Jacob his special place in the family for a bowl of stew. God's promise came true. The big brother served the little brother.

Esau was very angry,
because Jacob tricked him.

So Jacob was afraid,
and he ran away.

Jacob **ran**

and **ran**

and **ran.**

And after all that running,
Jacob was tired.

When the sun went down,
Jacob lay down on the ground,
and he went to sleep.

He put his head on a rock, because he didn't have a pillow.

Jacob had a dream.
In the dream,

God showed Jacob the way to heaven.

Jacob saw a giant staircase. It reached from the ground way up into the sky. Angels were walking up and down the stairs, and God was standing right at the top.

Do you know the way to heaven?

Everyone who trusts Jesus will live with God in heaven. Jesus is the way to heaven. Jesus will take God's people to the place where all God's promises are true all the time. Have you trusted in Jesus?

Then God spoke to Jacob, "Do you remember the promise I gave to your father, Isaac, and your grandfather, Abraham? I will give you more children than there are stars in the sky. I am with you, and I will take care of you wherever you go."

Jacob had twelve sons,
but Joseph was the favorite.

12
Can you count
the brothers?

Jacob gave Joseph a fancy coat with lots of colors. The other brothers
were jealous of that beautiful coat. They wanted one just like it.

Even though Joseph was a little brother, Jacob made him the boss of his older brothers. When the brothers would do something wrong, Joseph would tell on them.

That made the brothers
jealous and **angry.**
Was that good? No.

The brothers took care of their father's sheep. One day, Joseph went to check on them. When the brothers saw him coming, they said, "Let's get him."

Then the brothers tore off Joseph's coat, and they threw him into a hole in the ground.

Joseph was hurt and afraid.
Was that good? No.

Some traders came by with camels. One brother said, "Let's sell Joseph." The brothers did, and the traders took Joseph to Egypt. In Egypt, Joseph was a slave and went to prison. **Was that good? No.**

Lots of bad things happened to Joseph, but God was always with him. One day God gave Joseph the chance to help the king. The king was so grateful that he set Joseph free from prison and put him in charge of all of Egypt.

Then Joseph's family came to live in Egypt. God helped Joseph to forgive his brothers for hurting him.

They all lived happily together.

Was God's plan good? Yes!
Even when bad things happen,

God's plans are still **good.**

Do you trust God's plan?

Many years later one of Jesus's friends sold him. People put Jesus on a cross to die. Jesus's friend made a bad plan, but God's plans are still good. God wanted Jesus to die for our sins so that everyone who trusts him can be saved.

Joseph and his brothers had children, and their children had children. God's people began to fill up the land of Egypt.

After many years there was a new king of Egypt who didn't care about Joseph or his people. He didn't want God's people in his land! So he made a bad law.

He said, "Every baby boy from Joseph's family must be thrown into the river."

45

Miriam and her family were part of Joseph's family. Miriam's mother had a baby boy.

They all **loved** him so much!

Would Miriam's mother throw the baby into the river? No!

Miriam watched her mother
make a basket.

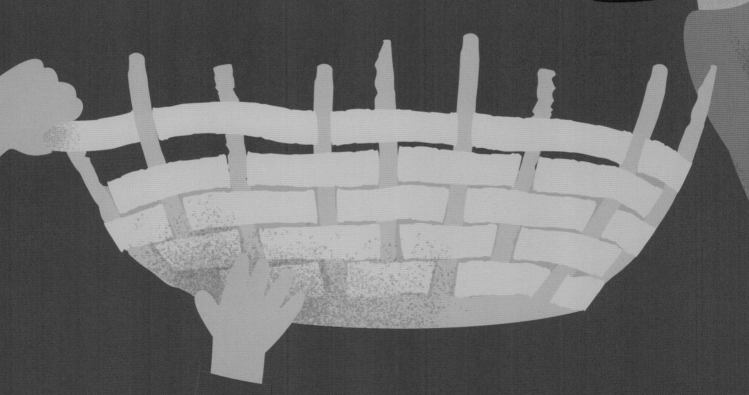

She wove it together tightly to keep
the water out. Then she sealed it with
sticky tar so it would float.

Miriam kept watching. Her mother put her baby brother in the basket. Then she hid it in the reeds beside the river. "Keep watching the basket," said Miriam's mother. Miriam obeyed.

What did she see? She saw a princess come to the river to take a bath. Miriam kept watching the basket. The princess heard the baby cry. What would she do?

Would the princess throw the baby into the river? No.

The princess loved the baby. "You will be my boy," she said. The princess named the baby Moses. Then she took Moses home to her beautiful palace. While Miriam was watching, God was watching too.

God watches over his people.

Who watches you and keeps you safe?

God watches over his people just like Miriam watched over Moses. God's people are safe with Jesus just like Moses was safe in the basket.

Moses grew up and left Egypt. The king was still being mean to Joseph's family, so Moses left the beautiful palace and the princess. He went to live far away and work as a shepherd.

One day, Moses was out in the country taking care of his sheep when he saw something very strange.

He saw a bush that was on fire, but there wasn't any smoke. The bush was burning, but the branches didn't turn black. The leaves didn't dry up. How could a bush be on fire but not burn up?

Then God spoke to Moses from inside the bush.

"My people are slaves in Egypt," said God,

"but I have a plan to rescue them. I'm sending you."

Moses was surprised and scared. "Me!?" he asked. Moses didn't like God's plan. "What if the king doesn't listen to me?" asked Moses.

Then God said, "Your job is to show the king my power."
God told Moses to throw his staff—his shepherd's stick—on
the ground. Moses obeyed. Right away the staff changed.

**It started to rattle . . .
and slither . . .
and hiss.**

It turned into a snake.
How could Moses's staff turn into a snake like that?
God changed the staff.

And God was with Moses.

God said, "I will go with you. I will change you
into a brave leader. I will teach you what to say."

Did you know?

God gave Moses his Holy Spirit. The Spirit made Moses into a great leader. God promises to give his people the Holy Spirit too. The Holy Spirit changes God's people so that they live like Jesus.

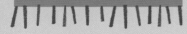

God's people were still slaves in Egypt, but God remembered his promise to rescue them. So God sent Moses to Pharaoh, the king of Egypt.

Moses said,
"God says, 'Let my people go.'"

But stubborn Pharaoh said No to God.

So Moses went down to the big river. He hit it with his staff. All the water in Egypt turned to blood.

Yuck!

NO!

No one had anything to drink. Then Moses said to Pharaoh again, "Let God's people go." But stubborn Pharaoh just said No.

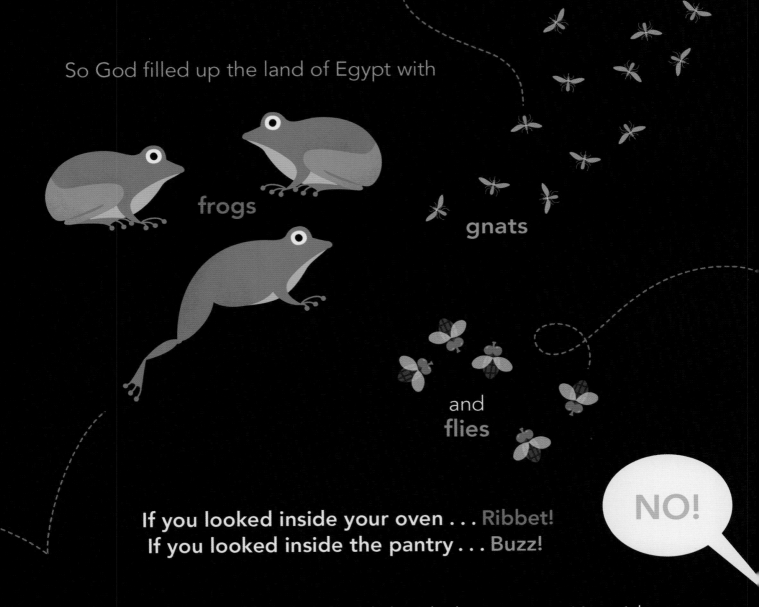

So God filled up the land of Egypt with

frogs

gnats

and
flies

NO!

If you looked inside your oven . . . Ribbet!
If you looked inside the pantry . . . Buzz!

Pharaoh changed his mind and decided to say yes. He said,
"Moses, *please* pray to God for me." Moses prayed, and God took
away the frogs and gnats and flies. But stubborn Pharaoh changed
his mind and would not let God's people go.

Then all the cows and sheep in Egypt got sick. People had sores on their bodies. God sent hail—ice from the sky. He sent grasshoppers to eat the people's food.

He covered all of Egypt with darkness.

Pharaoh started crying. "Oh Moses! I've made bad choices. I disobeyed God. Please stop these terrible plagues." God did stop the plagues, but then . . .

Stubborn Pharaoh shouted:

NO way! I will NOT let the people go.

Have you ever said No when you should have obeyed?

Sometimes we are stubborn like Pharaoh. But that can't stop God's promise. Jesus can save us from a stubborn heart.

61

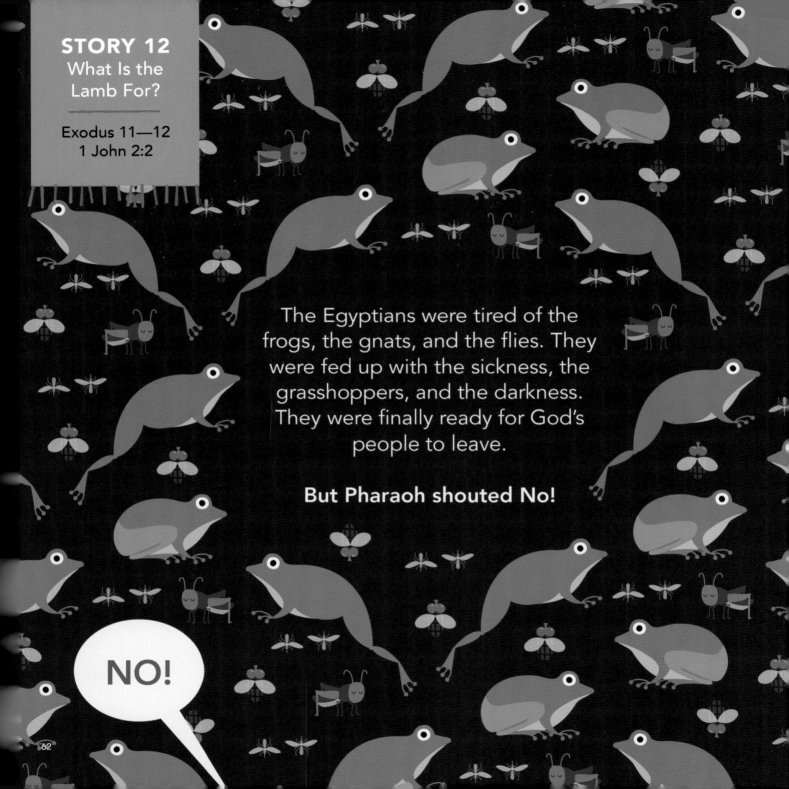

STORY 12
What Is the Lamb For?

Exodus 11—12
1 John 2:2

The Egyptians were tired of the frogs, the gnats, and the flies. They were fed up with the sickness, the grasshoppers, and the darkness. They were finally ready for God's people to leave.

But Pharaoh shouted No!

NO!

That was a terrible mistake. Moses said to Pharaoh, "This time, it won't be just frogs, gnats, and flies. This very night the oldest son from every family in Egypt will die—even yours.

But Pharaoh just kept saying No!

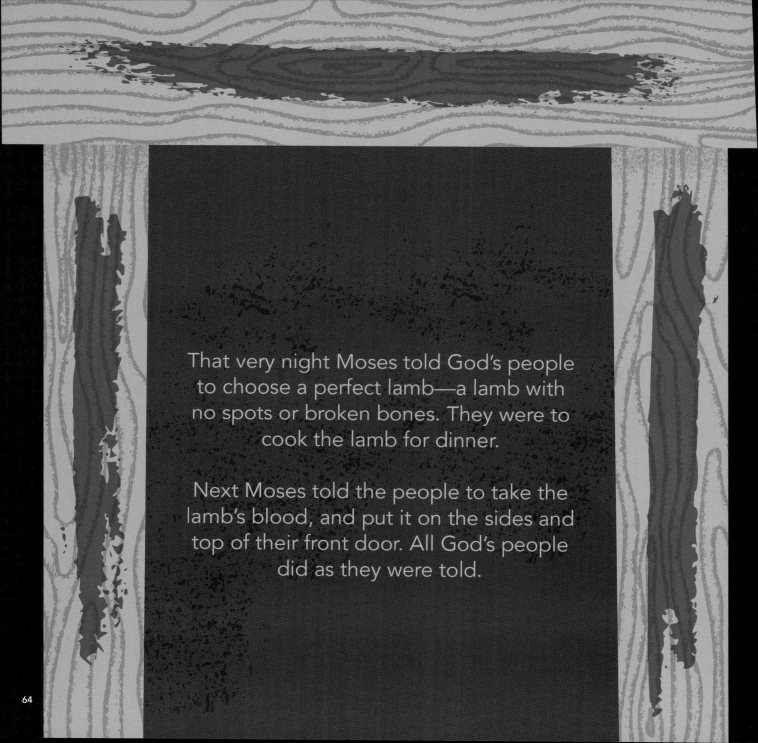

That very night Moses told God's people to choose a perfect lamb—a lamb with no spots or broken bones. They were to cook the lamb for dinner.

Next Moses told the people to take the lamb's blood, and put it on the sides and top of their front door. All God's people did as they were told.

The next morning Pharaoh cried. God's words that Moses had spoken had come true. Pharaoh's son had died, along with the oldest son in every Egyptian family. But the children of God's people were all safe. Now Pharaoh knew that God was more powerful than a king. Pharaoh finally said, "Yes. God's people can go."

YES.

God's people followed Moses's instructions.

In every home, little
children asked,
"What is this lamb for?"

This is what the parents said,

"The perfect lamb helps us remember God's promise to forgive.

This special meal is called the Passover, because God passed over our families and did not kill our oldest sons as he did in the homes of the Egyptians."

How does God keep his promise to forgive today?

Through Jesus. Jesus is the true Lamb of God. His blood paid for the sins of the world.

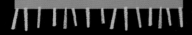

God's people left Egypt as *quickly* as they could.

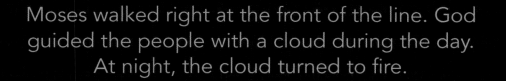

Moses walked right at the front of the line. God guided the people with a cloud during the day. At night, the cloud turned to fire.

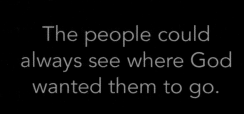

The people could always see where God wanted them to go.

Soon God's people came to the Red Sea.
It looked as big as an ocean.

There was
no way to walk
--- **across** --->
it.

They couldn't fly
over
it.

They couldn't dig
under
it.

E G Y P T

PHARAOH'S
ARMY

RED SEA

GOD'S PEOPLE

God's cloud stood still. The people stood still in the hot sun. They started to complain: "Moses, why did you bring us out here? It's too hot!"

Moses looked behind them. Pharaoh was coming with chariots and horses and his entire army. He was coming to take God's people back to Egypt. There was no way to escape.

God's people were afraid.
But Moses said,

"Be still. God will keep his promises.

God will fight for you."

Then God told Moses to stretch out his staff over the sea. Right away, the water separated. There were two giant walls of water, one on the left and one on the right. God's people walked right between the walls of water on dry ground.

God kept his people safe until they were
all the way across the sea. Then Moses
raised his staff over the sea again.

The water crashed down on Pharaoh and his army. That was the last God's people saw of them.

Have you ever been afraid?

When we are afraid, we can trust Jesus. Jesus is on our side. He fights for his people.

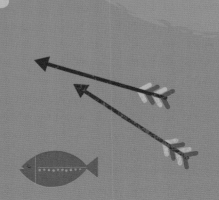

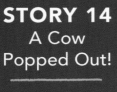
Moses took God's people to a big mountain. Then Moses climbed up the mountain, and God spoke to Moses for days and days.

UP!

He gave Moses his law and commandments on stone tablets. One of God's commandments said,

"Do NOT believe in or worship any pretend gods."

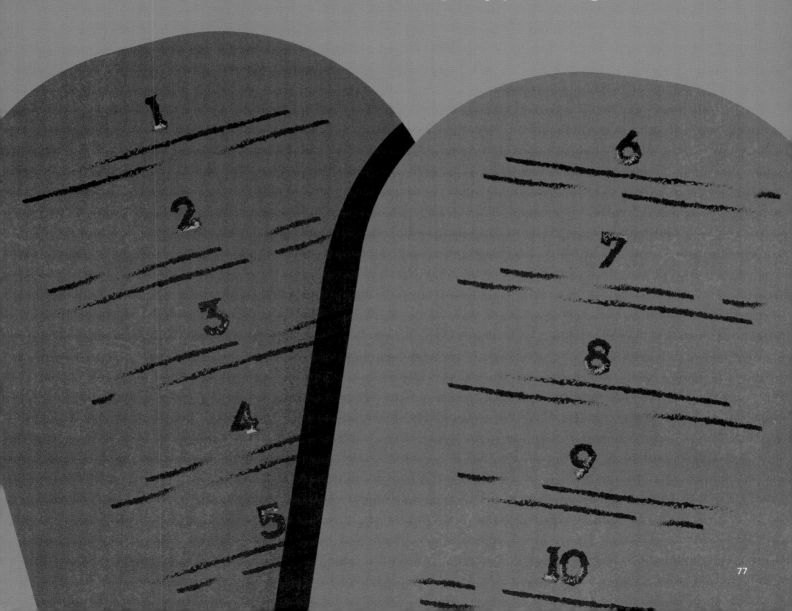

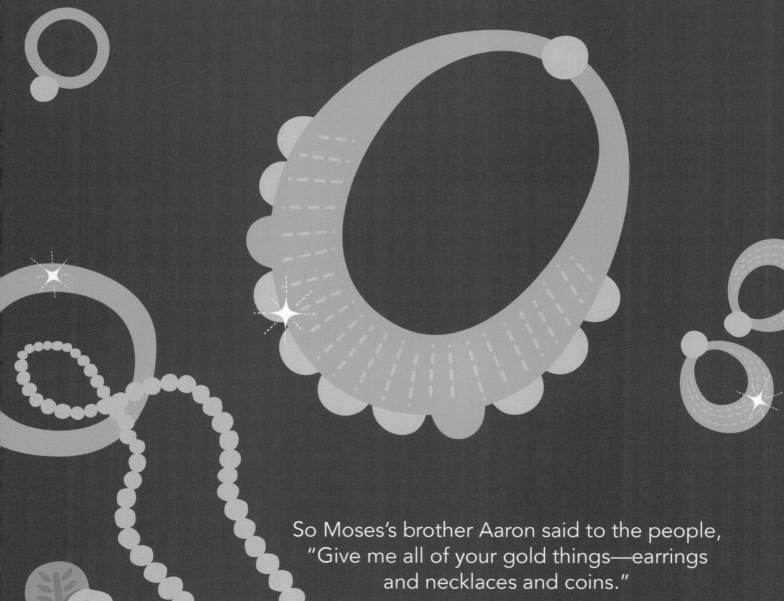

Moses stayed on the mountain for a long time. He stayed so long that the people worried he would not come back.

So Moses's brother Aaron said to the people, "Give me all of your gold things—earrings and necklaces and coins."

Aaron melted the gold in a fire and shaped it into
a baby cow—a golden calf.

Then the people had a
PARTY.

They praised and worshiped the golden calf and said,
"This is our god who saved us from Egypt!"

Oh no!
The people didn't love God best.

Oh no!
The people disobeyed God's law.

Moses hurried down the mountain with God's stone tablets.

DOWN!

Moses saw the people. He was angry with his brother Aaron. He threw the stone tablets to the ground, and they broke into pieces.

Then Moses said to Aaron, "What have you done? Why did you disobey God?" Aaron lied, "The people gave me the gold. I threw it into the fire. Then this calf just popped out!"

Now Moses was sad.

Moses prayed for the people.

He said, "God, don't forget about your promises. Please forgive the people's sin."

Have you ever been angry with your brother or sister or friend?

Instead of being angry when someone sins against us, we can choose to pray for them. We can pray, because Jesus prays for us when we sin too.

God's people walked and walked and walked. Finally they came to the new land God had promised Abraham a long, long, long time ago. They didn't know much about the land.

Were the people
who lived there

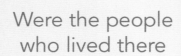

STRONG or weak?

Did they live in

small
towns

 or

BIG cities?

Was the food

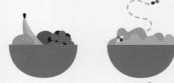

yummy or **yucky?**

Moses sent twelve men to find out everything about the new land.
They were called spies.

shh!!

The spies snuck around quietly
to see what the land was like.

When they came back, the spies told Moses,
"The food there is very good. The land is full of milk, honey,
and tasty fruit . . .

BUT it's too dangerous to live there.

The cities have high walls. And the people are giants.
They are so big they make us feel like grasshoppers!"

Ten of the spies shook with fear.
"Yikes," they cried, **"We're scared."**

The last two spies, Joshua and Caleb, trusted God.
"Don't be afraid," they said. "The people in the land are big,
but God is bigger. We can go in.

JOSHUA

We can be brave, because **God is with us."**

CALEB

The people had a choice to make. Would they listen to the
ten scared spies or would they listen to Joshua and Caleb?

The people made the wrong choice.
"Why did we come to this scary place?" the people cried.
They started to pack their bags.

They wanted to go back to Egypt.
But God didn't let them go back.

But God didn't let them
go into the land either.

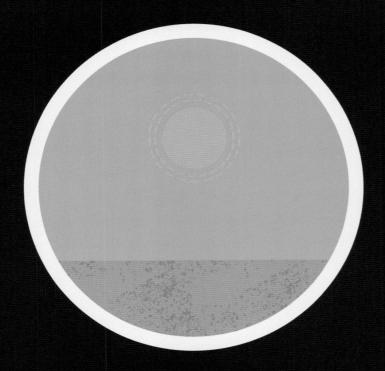

Because the people complained,
God made them stay in the
hot desert for forty more long years.

Have you ever done something brave?

Sometimes we disobey God because we are afraid to do what seems scary. But Jesus was always brave. He trusted God's plan. He died for our sins. Now we can be brave, because Jesus is with us.

God's people walked
around the desert for forty
more years. The desert was hot
and dry. The people were tired.

They complained
again and again.

God sent snakes into their camp. The snakes bit the people.
The snake bites made the people sick.

When the people got sick, they saw they had sinned
against God by complaining. They begged Moses,

"Save us! Take away the snakes."

Moses prayed to God,
but God didn't take away the snakes.

Instead, God told
Moses to make a
pretend snake.

God told Moses to
put the pretend
snake high up on a
stick so everyone
could see it.

Moses said, "Look up at the pretend snake and you will get well."
Everyone who had a snake bite looked up at the snake on a stick,
and they were saved from the sickness.

Everyone complains! We complain when we don't get our own way, when we have to share, and when we have to eat food we don't like.

Sometimes we even complain about God. Complaining is sin. God tells us that the punishment for sin is death.

But there is good news. Jesus said, "I am like Moses's pretend snake." Jesus hung high up on the cross.

Have you trusted in Jesus?

God loves the world so much that he sent Jesus. Everyone who trusts in Jesus will be saved from sin and live with God forever.

Everyone who looks to Jesus is saved from their sins—even the sin of complaining!

God saves everyone who trusts in Jesus.

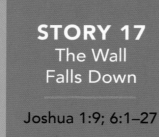

Finally God's people were ready to enter into their new land.
But they had enemies who didn't want to let them in. Their
enemies lived in big cities. One city was called Jericho. The
people of Jericho built a tall wall around their big city.

96

They locked up every door tight. No one came in or out of the city.

God spoke to Moses's helper, Joshua. God said, "I am giving you Jericho. It's part of the land I promised you. The people can lock their doors, but they can't keep you out. I will go with you. I will fight for you."

God told Joshua his plan. "Walk around the city quietly one time every day for six days.

On the seventh day, walk around the city seven times. After this, blow your horns and shout as loud as you can."

Joshua trusted God, and the people did exactly what God said. They marched around and around Jericho, one day, two days, three days, four days, five days, six days. On the seventh day, they blew their horns.

Pum-Pum-Pa-Pum!

The people shouted,

"Ahhhhhhh!"

Then the wall of the city crumbled and fell down flat.

Crash!

Why did God's people
win the battle?

Was it because they
marched around the city?

No.

Was it because they
blew their horns?

No.

Was it because they shouted?

No.

How are God's people saved from sin?

Does going to church save you from sin? Will reading your Bible save you from sin? Will praying save you from sin? No.

We can't do anything to save ourselves. Jesus defeats sin for his people. Only Jesus can save us from sin.

GOD knocked down the wall.
GOD gave Joshua the city.

GOD won the battle for his people.

Naomi lived in the Promised Land with her husband and two boys. They had no food. Naomi and her husband left the Promised Land and went to a new place where there was food to eat.

While they lived outside of God's land, Naomi's sons grew up and got married.

But then something sad happened. Naomi's
husband died. Naomi's sons died.

Naomi was sad. Naomi had lost everything.

But Naomi still had Ruth.
Ruth had been married to one of Naomi's sons.

FAMILY

Ruth said to Naomi, "I love you and want to stay with you. I will go wherever you go. I will live wherever you live. Your family will be my family. The true God you worship will be my God too."

Ruth and Naomi moved back to the Promised Land. Ruth took care of Naomi. She went to a farm where a man named Boaz lived. Ruth followed behind the workers in Boaz's fields to gather leftover grain. Then she took the grain home so Naomi could make bread.

Boaz watched Ruth when she came to his fields. He liked that she worked hard to take care of Naomi. Boaz was glad to help Ruth because he loved her. Ruth loved Boaz too. She knew another way Boaz could help her. She asked him, "Will you marry me?" Boaz said, "Yes!" So Boaz and Ruth were married and had a baby boy.

Naomi had been sad, but now she was happy. God had not forgotten her.

God gave Naomi a new family.

Did you know that Ruth was King David's great-grandmother?

Not only that. She was Jesus's great, great, far-off grandmother too. God gave Naomi and Ruth a new family. God gave them King Jesus too!

Many years later, a man named Elkanah lived in God's Promised Land. Elkanah's wife's name was Hannah, and he loved her very much. But Hannah was very sad, because she didn't have any children.

Hannah wanted to have a baby more than anything. She prayed again and again for God to give her a son.

She prayed and prayed.
She cried and cried.

Finally, Hannah made a promise, "God, please don't forget about me. If you will give me a son, I will give him back to you. He will work at God's house for all his life."

Hannah thought maybe God could not hear her. She thought maybe God had forgotten about her. But even if we feel forgotten,

God always listens to us.

And God listened to Hannah. God answered Hannah's prayer.

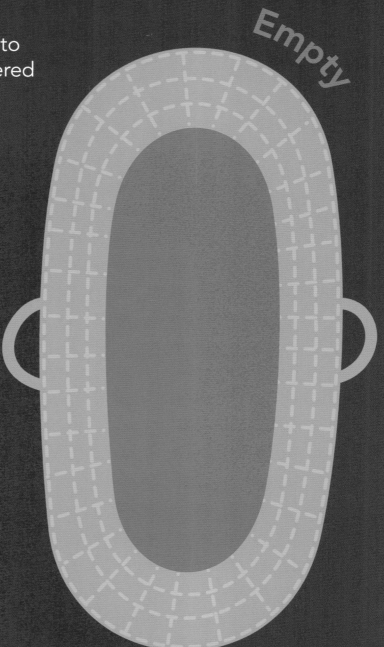

Empty

Very soon, Hannah had a baby boy. Hannah named her baby Samuel, which means "God listens."

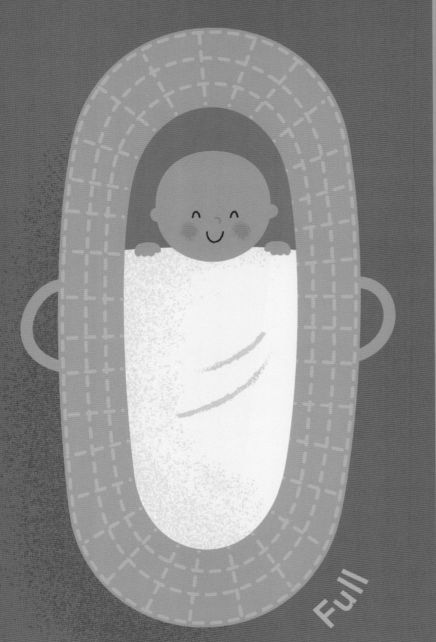

Full

Do you ever feel lonely or forgotten?

Even when we feel lonely, God's Spirit is with us. God does not forget about us. He listens when we pray. We can pray to him right now.

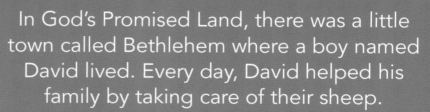

In God's Promised Land, there was a little town called Bethlehem where a boy named David lived. Every day, David helped his family by taking care of their sheep.

When lions or bears came to hurt the sheep, God helped David chase them away with his staff and sling.

David had lots of big brothers. They were soldiers who fought for God's people. One day David left the sheep so he could take some food to his brothers.

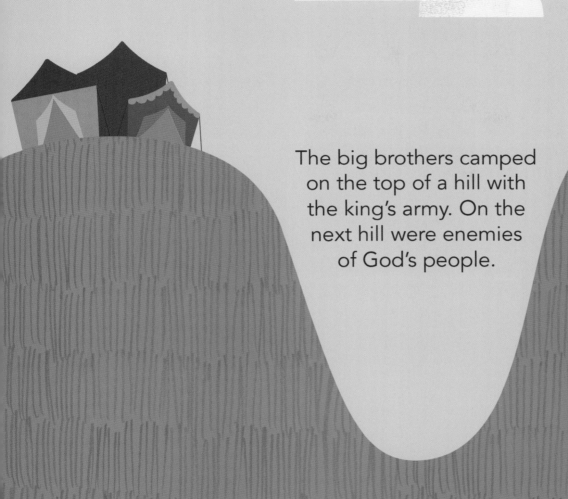

The big brothers camped on the top of a hill with the king's army. On the next hill were enemies of God's people.

In the enemy army was a giant named Goliath.

He was huge!

T
A
L
L

He was dressed from head to toe in heavy armor.
He carried a big sword and a giant spear.

Every day Goliath shouted,
"Choose one of your soldiers to come fight me."

When God's people heard Goliath, they were afraid. Even the king was afraid. David was little, but when David heard the giant, he was not afraid. David said, "Don't be afraid.

We can trust God to save us.

SHORT

God will help me fight Goliath."

Goliath had armor and a big sword.

David had just a small sling.

David put a stone in his sling
and swung it around.

The rock hit Goliath right in the middle of his forehead. The giant crashed to the ground and died. When the enemies saw that Goliath was dead, they ran away.

What kinds of things are scary to you?

David fought against a scary giant. But he trusted God to save him. When we feel afraid, we can trust Jesus. Jesus saves us.

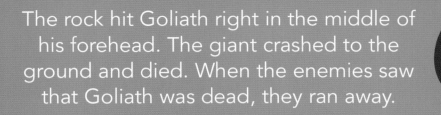

STORY 21
David and
Jonathan
Are Friends

1 Samuel 18—20
Proverbs 17:17
John 15:15

God's people loved David.
They told stories about how great David was.

They even sang songs about him.

120

But King Saul didn't love David.
King Saul was jealous.

He wanted the people to tell stories
and sing songs about him instead.

Every time God helped David win
another battle, Saul became more
jealous and angry.

King Saul had a son named Prince Jonathan. Prince Jonathan was kind to David. He decided to be David's friend.

David was afraid of King Saul, because King Saul was so jealous and angry. But Jonathan wanted to help David and protect him.

He promised David, "I will help you get away from jealous King Saul. I will always be your friend."

A friend loves you
all the time.

The two friends made a plan. David found a good hiding place in a field, and he waited. Jonathan came out to the field early in the morning and shot three arrows into the sky. This was Jonathan's signal to David. Jonathan told David that King Saul was very angry. He warned David to run away and hide.

Even after David became king of all Israel, he never forgot how his friend Jonathan had helped him.

Who is your best friend?

Jesus is the king. King Jesus decided to be our friend. Jesus loves us all the time.

STORY 22
Solomon
Chooses Wisely

1 Kings 10
2 Chronicles 1
Matthew 12:42
James 1:5

King David had a son named Solomon. After David died, God made Solomon the next king. God told Solomon, "Ask me for anything you want and I will give it to you."

Solomon could have asked for lots of **money**.

But he didn't.

Solomon could have asked for lots of **houses and land**.

But he didn't.

Solomon wanted to be a good king like his father, so Solomon asked God for **wisdom** to make right choices.

God gives wisdom to **everyone** who asks.

Solomon asked for **wisdom** and God said Yes!

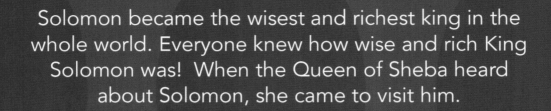

Solomon became the wisest and richest king in the whole world. Everyone knew how wise and rich King Solomon was! When the Queen of Sheba heard about Solomon, she came to visit him.

She brought camels carrying all kinds of gifts to his palace.

There were gold,
spices, diamonds,
and rubies.

The queen sat down and asked Solomon
lots of really hard questions.

Solomon answered every one of them! Nothing was too hard for Solomon to explain. The Queen of Sheba was amazed!

Who should we talk to when we need wisdom?

People came from far away just to listen to Solomon and hear his wise words. But we know someone who is even wiser than Solomon. Jesus is our wise king. He gives wisdom as a free gift to everyone who asks.

STORY 23
Jeremiah Is
Thrown into a Pit

Jeremiah 38:1–13
Lamentations 3:22–24
Psalm 40:1–3

After Solomon died, there were many **bad kings.**

132

They and God's people forgot about God and God's rules. God sent prophets to warn them, "Stop sinning and trust the one true God."

One of God's prophets was Jeremiah.
The king's royal helpers didn't like Jeremiah.
It made them mad when Jeremiah told them
they were disobeying God.

They put their hands over
their ears and shouted,

Stop telling us
God will punish us.
**We don't want to hear
that bad news!**

The angry helpers made an evil plan. They threw Jeremiah into a deep pit. Jeremiah fell down into the pit and landed in the mud.

PLOP!

The pit was slimy and deep. Jeremiah was sinking. He couldn't get out! Jeremiah needed someone to help him.

God shows **mercy** to his people.

God sent a friend to rescue Jeremiah from the pit.

A servant from the palace came to help Jeremiah. He found thirty men to help him lower ropes down for Jeremiah. They carefully lifted Jeremiah out of the pit.

Can you think of a time when you needed help?

God shows mercy to his people. God rescues us when we cannot help ourselves.

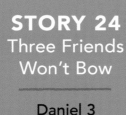

STORY 24
Three Friends
Won't Bow

Daniel 3
Psalm 145:3
Jeremiah 9:24

God's people didn't listen to God, so they had to leave their land and be slaves in a new land ruled by King Nebuchadnezzar. King Nebuchadnezzar was the mightiest king in the whole world. One day, King Nebuchadnezzar said, "Build a giant golden statue. Make it ninety feet tall. Make it look exactly like ME."

Next the king gathered all his musicians. "Grab your horns, flutes, guitars, harps, and bagpipes. I want you to play a song. A song about ME."

Then the king made a law. "Whenever you hear MY song, everyone must bow down and worship MY golden statue!" The King loved to hear people say he was THE GREATEST.

Everyone in the kingdom bowed down and worshiped King Nebuchadnezzar's statue. Everyone, that is, except for three brave friends who were part of God's people. The three friends were Shadrach, Meshach, and Abednego.

When King Nebuchadnezzar heard that these friends were not bowing down to worship his statue, he was furious. He said to them, "You must bow down. If you don't, I'll throw you into a blazing fire."

Shadrach, Meshach, and Abednego trusted God. They told the king, "You are mighty, but God is MIGHTIER. Your statue is big, but God is BIGGER.

God is the mightiest and the best.

God can rescue us from the fire. But even if he doesn't, we will not worship you or your golden statue. We will only worship GOD."

The friends' answer made King Nebuchadnezzar furious. He threw Shadrach, Meshach, and Abednego into the fire.

But God sent his angel to protect the three friends. The angel stopped the fire from burning them. Not even their hair or their clothes got burned.

King Nebuchadnezzar was amazed. Instead of bragging about himself, he started bragging about God. He said, "Praise the MIGHTY GOD of Shadrach, Meshach, and Abednego. God has rescued them from the blazing fire!"

We can brag about God too!

We can brag about Jesus! Praise Jesus for rescuing his people. Praise Jesus because HE is the mightiest and the best.

King Xerxes ruled Persia.
He married a young girl
named Esther. Esther was
one of God's people,
but no one knew that.
She kept it a secret.

Esther had an uncle named Mordecai who loved her. One day Mordecai heard terrible news. He heard that the king's royal helper, Haman, made a wicked plan to kill all of God's people.

God's people needed help!

hhhhhh!!!!!!

God's people needed someone to speak up for them.

They needed someone to tell the king about Haman's wicked plan.

Mordecai knew who could help God's people. Esther could speak up for God's people!

Queen Esther could tell the king her secret. If King Xerxes knew that Esther was part of God's family, he would not let Haman do this terrible thing.

But Esther was afraid. "What if King Xerxes is angry when I come to him?" thought Esther. "What if the king wants to kill me when he finds out I'm part of God's people?"

Esther asked Mordecai to pray for her. Esther asked God's people to pray for her. Then she went to see the king.

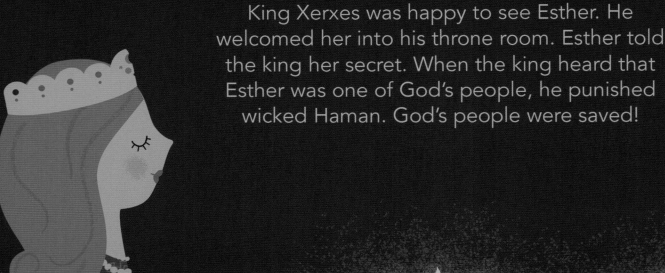

King Xerxes was happy to see Esther. He welcomed her into his throne room. Esther told the king her secret. When the king heard that Esther was one of God's people, he punished wicked Haman. God's people were saved!

Have you ever been afraid to speak up for someone else?

We can be brave and speak up to help others, because Jesus speaks up for us. Jesus speaks to God the Father for us just like Esther spoke to King Xerxes for God's people.

It was time for God's people to return home. But when they arrived, the land was a mess. The city of Jerusalem was destroyed. The city walls had fallen down. The city gates had been burned in a fire.

When Nehemiah heard about Jerusalem's broken walls and burned up gates, he was very sad. "If more enemies come, there are no walls to protect God's people," he thought. Nehemiah began to cry. Did God forget his promises? Did God stop loving his people?

Even though Nehemiah was sad, he still trusted God. Nehemiah prayed, "God, please remember your promises. Please be kind to your people. Please help us clean up Jerusalem and build the city walls again."

God **listens** when we are sad.

He heard Nehemiah's prayer.

152

Here's how God answered Nehemiah's prayer. Nehemiah's job was to help the king. One day while Nehemiah was bringing the king his cup, the king asked Nehemiah, "Why are you so sad?"

Nehemiah answered, "I'm sad, because my people's city is a mess. The city wall is broken down, and the gates have been burned with fire."

What do you think the king said?

The king told Nehemiah that he wanted to help! The king told Nehemiah to go to Jerusalem and rebuild the city wall.

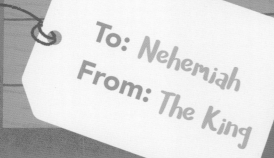

The king even gave Nehemiah the wood and other supplies he would need to build the wall.

He sent his army to keep Nehemiah and the workers safe.

To: Nehemiah
From: The King

Can you think of a time when you needed help?

We can talk to Jesus when we need help. God heard Nehemiah's prayer and made sure that the king helped his people. God listens to us, and he wants to help.

NEW
TESTAMENT

PROMISES KEPT

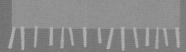

God's people had been waiting many years for the Savior God had promised. With every baby boy born the people wondered if this baby was the Savior.

young

Zechariah and Elizabeth were part of God's people. They were both very old, and they didn't have any children. But they loved God, obeyed him, and kept on waiting for God's promises.

old

God helps us believe and wait.

Zechariah worked in God's house, the temple. One special day, one of God's angels appeared and spoke to Zechariah. The angel said, "God will give you the baby boy you've been praying for. You must name him John. He will get God's people ready for the Savior."

Zechariah was shocked! He said, "We are too old to have a baby. How can we know God's promise really will come true?"

The angel answered,
"This is how you will know. God will make it
so you can't talk until the baby boy is born."

Zechariah tried to answer the angel,
but no sound came from his mouth.

Zechariah couldn't talk!

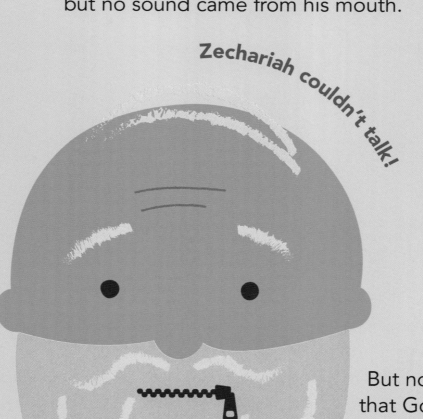

But now he believed
that God really would
give them a baby boy.

162

When the baby was born, some friends thought Zechariah and Elizabeth should name the boy Zechariah after his dad. But Zechariah remembered what the angel had said. He wrote, "His name is John." Right away, Zechariah started talking . . . and singing! He sang, "Our waiting is almost over. God is sending the Savior!"

Have you ever had to wait a long time?

It's hard to wait when we're standing in line. It's hard to wait for your birthday. It's hard to wait for Christmas. Sometimes we have to wait for God too. God helps us wait, remember, and believe that his promises always come true.

163

Finally, the day came when God's promise to send a Savior came true. It happened this way: God sent an angel to a young woman named Mary and told her that she would be the Savior's mother. God himself would be the Savior's father.

While the Savior, Jesus, was still in her tummy, Mary traveled with her husband, Joseph, to Bethlehem.

When they got there, the little town was crowded. They could not find a place to stay. Every room was full of people.

Someone was sleeping in every bed.

ZZZZZZZZZZZ...

165

The only place Mary and Joseph could find to rest was in a stable for animals. So Jesus wasn't born in a castle.

Jesus didn't sleep in a cozy crib. Jesus was born in a stable and he slept in a manger, a feeding box for cows and sheep.

That same night, God sent an army of angels to announce the good news to poor shepherds watching their sheep. The dark fields filled with light and the shepherds were very afraid. But an angel said, "Don't be scared. I have wonderful news! Jesus, the Savior, is born!

God is with us."

The shepherds hurried to find baby Jesus.

When they found him, they were so happy. They praised God and told everyone they could. Mary was amazed too. She remembered everything that happened and treasured the memory in her heart.

Will you share this good news?

God is with us. Jesus's birth is good news and great joy for all people. On that wonderful day, Jesus was born. Jesus is God. Jesus is our Creator who made everything. Jesus is the King of God's people, and he rules over everything too. Jesus, our great God, was born as a little baby! We can tell the good news to our friends. Think of a friend who you can tell the good news to.

After Jesus was born, some wise men from the East came to visit him. They stopped in Jerusalem and went to visit King Herod.

They asked the king, "Where is the new baby who is the King of God's people? We saw his star up in the sky, and we have some gifts for him!"

King Herod did not know that Jesus had been born. Herod felt angry inside. He did not like this news!

"God's people don't need a new king," he thought, "I'm the king. People should bring ME presents."

King Herod told the wise men a sneaky lie. He said, "When you find this new king, come tell me where he is. Then I can bring him a gift too." But Herod didn't want to bring Jesus a present, Herod wanted to find Jesus so he could kill him.

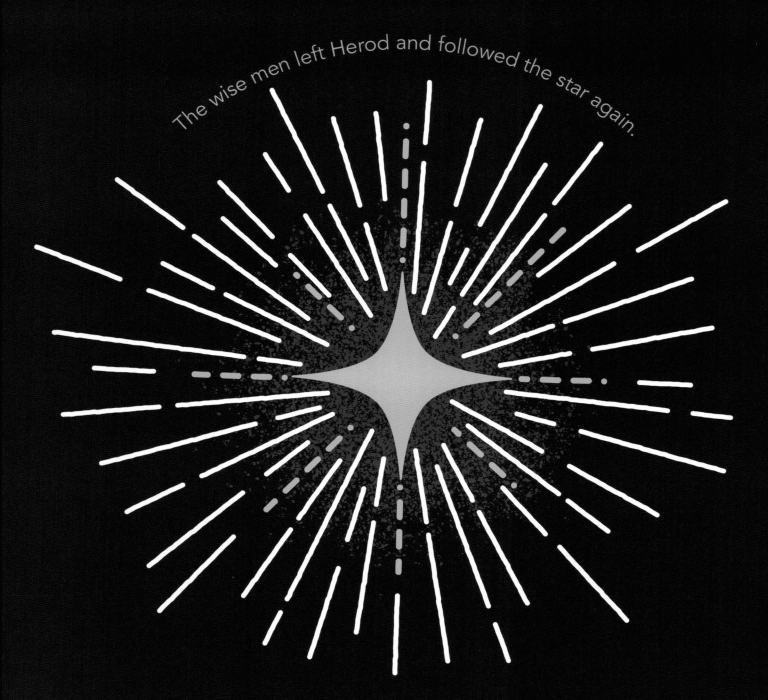

The wise men left Herod and followed the star again.

It led them to Jesus.

Did you know?
Jesus is the best king.

He is not selfish or jealous. His love is so great that it stretches up to the stars, and it reaches from east to west.

As soon as the wise men saw Jesus, they bowed down low and gave Jesus gold, sweet oil, and spices—rich gifts fit for a king.

That night, God spoke to the wise men in a dream. God told them not to tell jealous Herod where Jesus was. So the wise men got up and traveled back home a different way.

Jesus grew up with his parents and brothers and sisters. Did you know that Jesus was once a child like you?

The biggest difference is that

Jesus is God's Son,

and Jesus is perfect.

He never disobeyed. He never pulled his sisters' hair. He never got angry with his brothers. Even as a little child, Jesus always obeyed God.

176

Each year Jesus and lots of his family and friends went to Jerusalem to visit God's house and bring a gift for God.

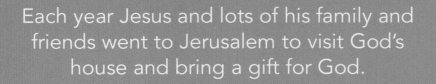

There were no cars or trains so they would

walk and walk. . .

for a whole week to get there.

One year, when Jesus was twelve years old, the whole family visited Jerusalem like they did every year. After their visit, Joseph and Mary started the long walk home.

They walked for a whole day and were setting up tents for the night when Mary and Joseph realized Jesus was missing.

left

outside

Mary looked to the right and she looked to the left. No Jesus! Joseph looked inside the tents. He looked where the donkeys and camels were resting. No Jesus! Mary and Joseph asked their friends,

"Have you seen Jesus?"
But no one knew where he was.

inside

right

So Joseph and Mary went quickly all the way back to Jerusalem looking for Jesus. Finally they found him.

Jesus was at God's house listening to the teachers and answering their questions. Mary said, "We've been looking everywhere for you!" But Jesus answered, "Why did you have to look for me? I always obey God, my Father. You should have known I would be at my Father's house."

What makes Jesus different from every other child?

We disobey our parents. We are selfish and often unkind to our brothers and sisters. But Jesus is perfect, because Jesus is God's Son. He always obeyed God the Father.

STORY 31
John Says,
"Turn Around!"

Matthew 3:1–12
Mark 1:3–8
Luke 3:2–17
John 1:19–34

When Zechariah and Elizabeth's son, John, grew up, he became a prophet just as the angel had said. A prophet is someone who tells people what God says.

John told God's people about Jesus's new kingdom.

John was very strange. He lived in the desert. He wore camel hair clothes.

And he ate bugs!

But the strangest thing about John was what God told him to say. Do you know what God told him to say?

John said, "Repent! Turn around!" And he said it again and again. Over and over, John kept saying the same thing: "Turn around!"

Some people think that being the boss will make you happy.

Some people think that having lots of money or toys will make you happy.

Some people think that being famous and having people say nice things about you will make you happy.

But John knew that none of those things will make us happy. Only Jesus can make us truly happy.

So John said, "Turn around!

Turn away from sin and turn to Jesus.

He is better than anything else."

Many people listened to John and turned to God. So John baptized them in the Jordan River. One day, while John was baptizing, he saw someone walking toward him in the crowd.

John pointed to him and said to the people, "Turn around! It's Jesus. He is the One who will save the world from sin."

How do people enter God's kingdom?

We must TURN AROUND!
We must turn away from sin
and trust in Jesus to save us.

Have you ever been to a party? One day Jesus went with his family and friends to a wedding party. They ate and drank and then they ate and drank some more. The wedding party didn't only last for a couple of hours. It went on for a whole week!

Everyone was having a wonderful time until . . .
the party ran out of wine.

Oh no!

empty   full

Imagine you went to a birthday party, but the cake was all
eaten up before you got a piece. How sad! The people at
the wedding party were sad too.

Jesus's mom knew that Jesus could help.
She told the party helpers,
"Do whatever Jesus tells you to do."

Jesus pointed to some
big stone jars.

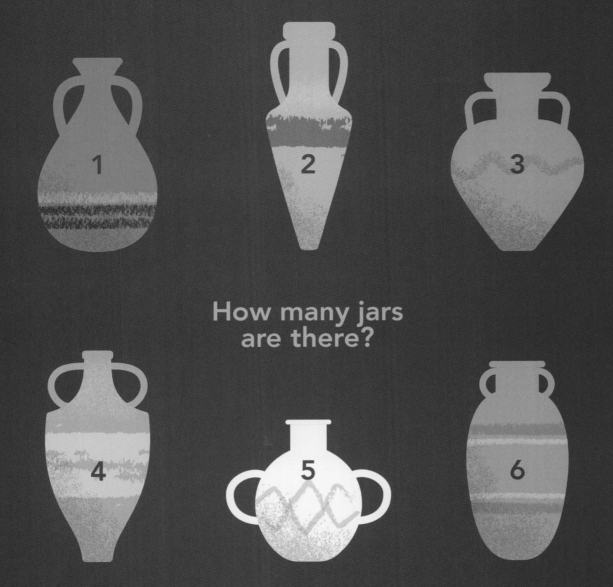

How many jars are there?

Jesus told the helpers, "Fill the jars with water." The helpers filled the jars full of water, right to the top. Then Jesus said, "Take some of the water from these jars and give it to the person in charge of the party."

But when the person in charge of the party tasted the water, he was surprised! It wasn't water at all. It was delicious wine!

Hooray! Jesus is **good** and **powerful.**

Jesus had turned the water into the very best wine.

Why do we celebrate and throw parties?

We celebrate holidays like Christmas and Easter. We celebrate birthdays with games and presents. But best of all, we celebrate Jesus, because he is good and powerful!

Jesus had a friend named Peter.
Peter was a fisherman.

One day, Jesus sat in Peter's boat and taught a large crowd of people who were standing on the shore. When he was done teaching, Jesus told Peter, "Row your boat out into the deep, deep water. Let's throw out your fishing nets and catch some fish!"

Peter said, "My friends and I worked hard all night trying to catch some fish, but we caught nothing! Our boats are completely empty."

194

Even though Peter didn't think he would catch any fish, he obeyed Jesus anyway. The fishermen rowed the boat out to the deep, deep water. They threw out their fishing nets. Then they began to pull the nets in. Do you think there were any fish in the nets?

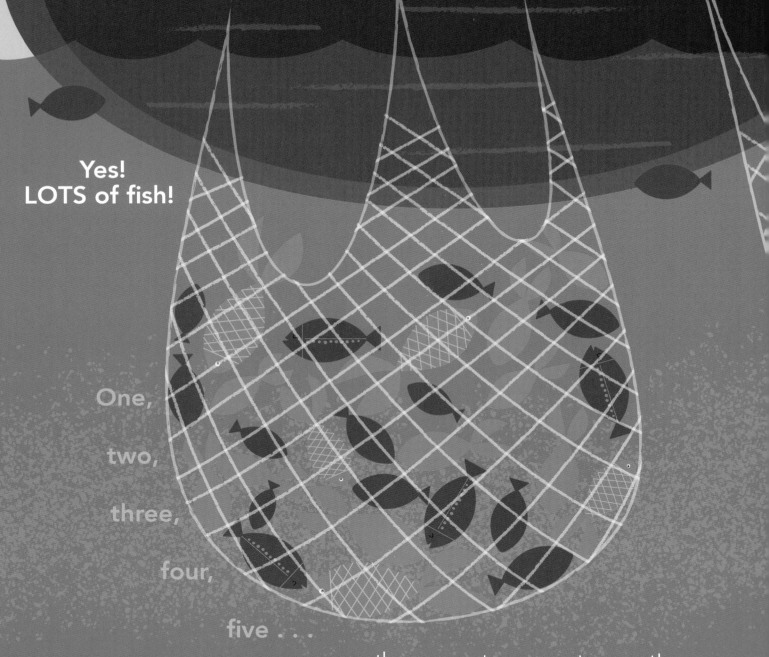

**Yes!
LOTS of fish!**

One,

two,

three,

four,

five . . .

there were too many to count!

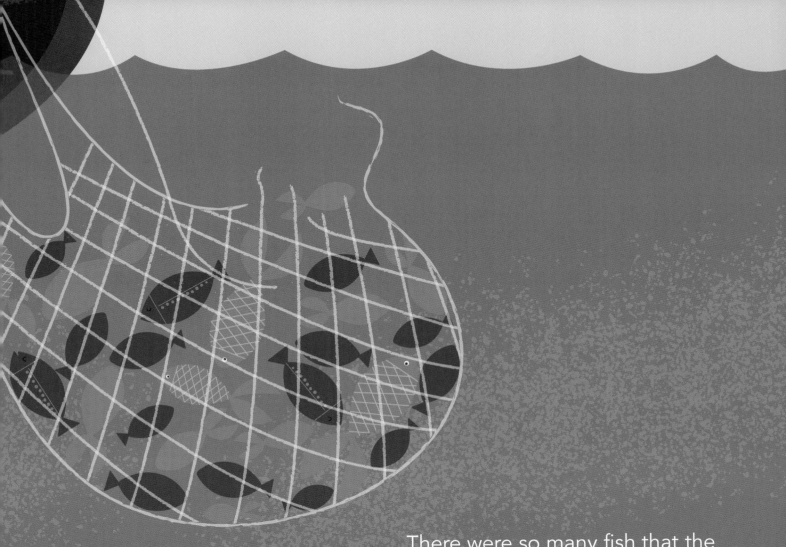

There were so many fish that the
nets started to break!

Peter's boat was piled high with fish. There were so many fish that a second boat was filled full too.

There were so many fish that the two boats started to sink.

Oh my!

Peter was amazed! Jesus is truly God. Even the fish obeyed him.

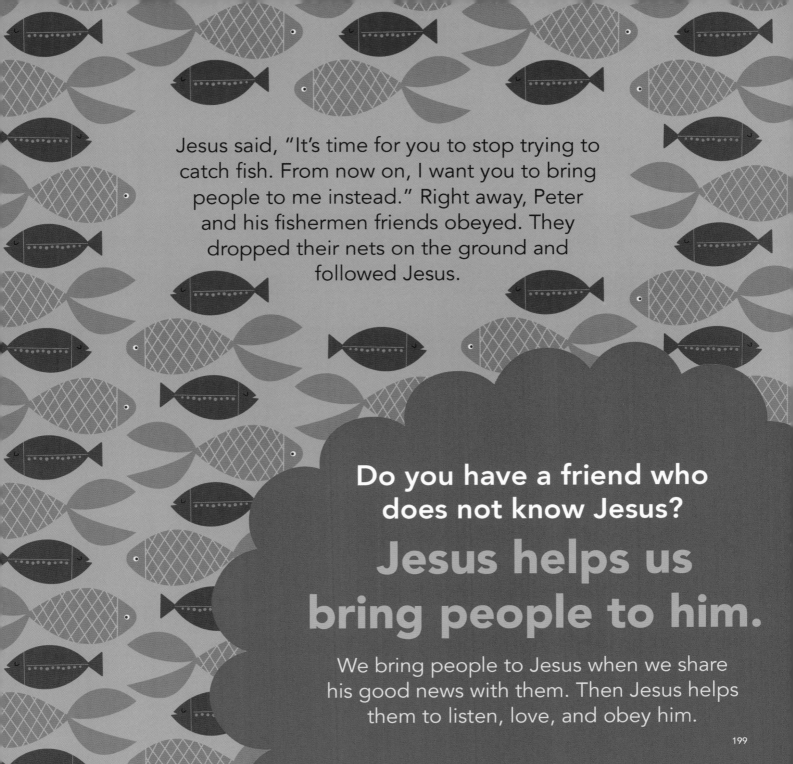

Jesus said, "It's time for you to stop trying to catch fish. From now on, I want you to bring people to me instead." Right away, Peter and his fishermen friends obeyed. They dropped their nets on the ground and followed Jesus.

Do you have a friend who does not know Jesus?

Jesus helps us bring people to him.

We bring people to Jesus when we share his good news with them. Then Jesus helps them to listen, love, and obey him.

STORY 34
Jesus Calms
The Sea

Matthew 8:23–27
Mark 4:36–41
Luke 8:22–25

One day, while Jesus and his friends sailed in a boat on a big lake, Jesus laid down to take a nap. Soon he was fast asleep.

Suddenly there was a thunderstorm.

Rain poured down
(pitter-patter, pitter-patter).

**Lightning flashed.
Thunder boomed.
Wind howled.**

Waves crashed against the boat.

SPLASH!

The storm was so scary! Jesus's friends were afraid.
But Jesus kept on sleeping.

"Jesus, wake up!" shouted Peter and his friends.
"We're going to drown!"

Jesus woke up and looked at his friends.
"Why are you so afraid?" he asked.
Then Jesus spoke to the storm,
"Stop. Be still."

Right away, the wind stopped howling. The rain stopped falling.

The thunder stopped booming. The waves stopped splashing.

Everything was calm.

Peter and his
friends were amazed!

Jesus is truly God.

Even the storm obeyed him.

Who do you call when you are afraid?

When you are afraid, you might call for your mom or
dad. But you can also call on Jesus. Jesus is truly God.
Even scary things obey Jesus.

Some of the leaders of God's people were called Pharisees. The Pharisees thought they were better than everyone else. They thought they could please God by trying hard to do lots of good things.

One day Jesus told this story. A Pharisee went to the temple to pray. He started praying, but really he was just bragging to God.

He said, "God, I read my Bible and pray every day. I give so much money to your temple. I am not like bad people who lie and steal and cheat. I'm so good!"

The Pharisee felt
PROUD.

He thought he could be
good without God's help.

That same day another man went to the temple. He was a tax collector. A tax collector's job was to collect money from people to give to the king.

But the tax collectors also cheated and stole more money to keep for themselves. No matter how much money a tax collector took, he always wanted more!

But when this tax collector prayed, he didn't start bragging. He found a corner and bowed his head. The tax collector cried and said, "God, I'm a **BIG SINNER**. Please forgive me for the bad things I have done."

The tax collector felt **SAD**.

He was sorry about his sin. He knew that he needed God's help.

What do you think happened? God was not happy with the Pharisee who bragged, but he forgave the tax collector.

All sin should be punished. God's punishment for sin is death. But Jesus came to rescue sinners from punishment and death.

Jesus came to save people who know they are sinners and who ask God for forgiveness.

How did Jesus feel about the tax collector?

Jesus was **HAPPY**.
Jesus loved the tax collector. Jesus loves to rescue sinners like you and me.

STORY 36
Jesus Heals the Blind Man

Mark 10:46–52
Luke 18:35–43
Isaiah 29:18

Bartimaeus couldn't see the road, so his friends had to hold his hands and show him where to walk. Every day, Bartimaeus walked with his friends to a place outside the city gate. Bartimaeus sat down there, and he begged the people who passed by to give him money.

"I'm a poor blind man," Bartimaeus said. "I cannot see to do work and earn money. Will you help me?"

One day, there were a LOT of people passing by
Bartimaeus. They bumped into him and made lots of noise.
"What's going on?" Bartimaeus wondered aloud. His friends
told him, "Jesus is coming down the road."

Bartimaeus was excited to hear that Jesus was coming. He started crying out, "Jesus, help me!" His friends were embarrassed. They told Bartimaeus to be quiet. Shhhh!

Shhhh!!!!!!

But Bartimaeus kept shouting louder and louder and LOUDER,

Jesus, help me!
JESUS, HELP ME!

Jesus stopped. He called Bartimaeus over and asked, "How can I help you?" Bartimaeus answered, "I want to see."

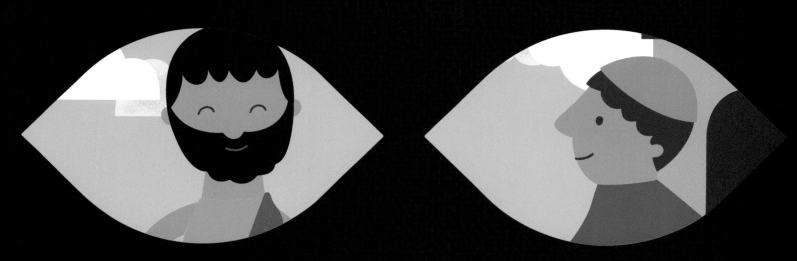

Jesus can heal sick people.

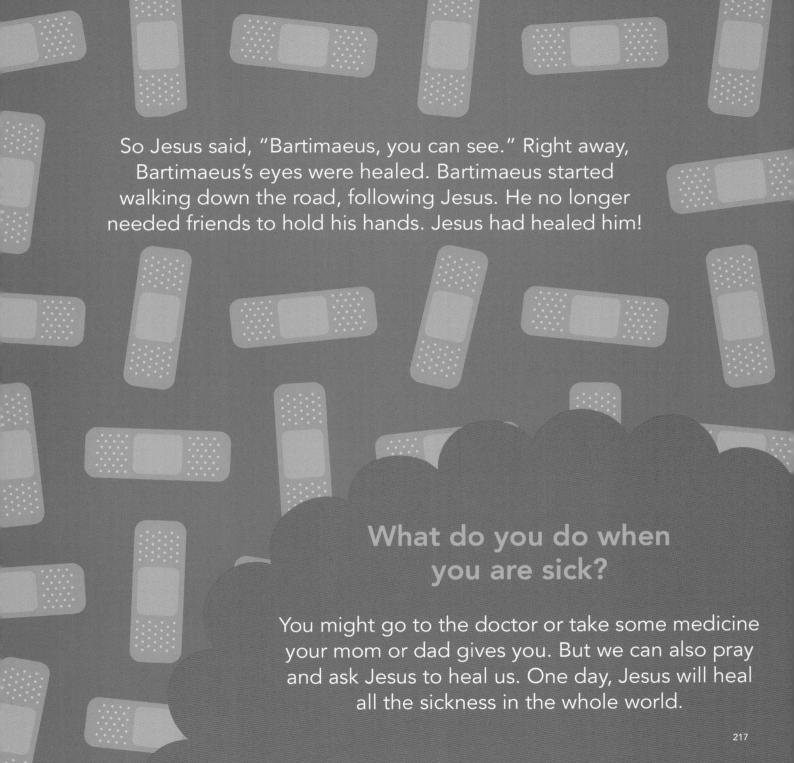

So Jesus said, "Bartimaeus, you can see." Right away, Bartimaeus's eyes were healed. Bartimaeus started walking down the road, following Jesus. He no longer needed friends to hold his hands. Jesus had healed him!

What do you do when you are sick?

You might go to the doctor or take some medicine your mom or dad gives you. But we can also pray and ask Jesus to heal us. One day, Jesus will heal all the sickness in the whole world.

Do you remember what tax collectors were like in Jesus's day? Tax collectors gathered money for the king. They were rich because they also cheated and stole more money to keep for themselves.

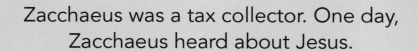

Zaccheus was a tax collector. One day, Zaccheus heard about Jesus.

He heard that
Jesus came to save big sinners—
even tax collectors!

Zaccheus wanted to see if it was true, so he went looking for Jesus.

Jesus had come to town and right away was surrounded by crowds of people. But Zacchaeus was a short man. He was too short to see over the people's heads.

Then Zacchaeus had an idea. He ran down the road ahead of the crowd to a tall tree. He climbed up high.

Then Zacchaeus sat up high in the tree where he could see over the heads of the crowd.

What do you think
Zacchaeus saw? He saw all
the men and the women and
the boys and the girls in the crowd.
Could Zacchaeus find JESUS?

**Can you see Jesus
in the picture?**

If you look for Jesus, he will find you.

Surprise! Jesus came to the tree where Zacchaeus was sitting. Jesus looked up and said, "Zacchaeus, I've been looking for you! I'm coming to your house today."

Are you looking for Jesus?

Zacchaeus was looking for Jesus, but Jesus found him! You can look for Jesus as you pray, as you read about him in the Bible, and as you listen to people tell you about him.

Zacchaeus scrambled down from the tree and went with Jesus. They walked to Zacchaeus's house and ate a meal together. Zacchaeus was so happy to find Jesus that he gave money to the poor. He paid back even more than what he had stolen.

Everywhere Jesus went, people gathered around him. Sometimes the people brought their children to see Jesus too.

Jesus would sit with the children and pray for them and show them his love.

One day, a group of children ran up to Jesus, but Jesus's friends held out their hands. "STOP!" they said. "Jesus is very busy. He has many important things to do. Jesus needs to teach the grownups. Jesus needs to heal sick people. Jesus does not have time for children."

But Jesus's friends were wrong.

Jesus loves little children.

He is not too busy to help them!
Jesus said, "Let the little children come to me.
Do not stop them from coming!"

Jesus wants even the youngest and smallest children to come to him.

biggest

oldest

In fact, Jesus said,
"My kingdom belongs to people
who are just like these children."

smallest

youngest

Will you come to Jesus?

You can pray and talk to Jesus anytime. You're not too little. Jesus is not too busy. Jesus loves talking with you. Jesus loves little children.

Once there was a family with one brother,
Lazarus, and two sisters, Martha and Mary.
They were Jesus's friends, and he loved them.

One day, Lazarus got sick. He was so sick that his sisters were afraid he would die. So Martha and Mary sent a letter to Jesus. The letter said,

Dear Jesus—

We need your help! Lazarus is very sick. Please come and heal him!

Then the sisters waited for Jesus.

Martha and Mary waited and waited. While they waited for Jesus, Lazarus got sicker and sicker until one day he died. Martha and Mary were very sad.

Finally, Jesus arrived at Mary and Martha's town. One at a time, the sisters came to see Jesus. They both said the same thing: "Lazarus is already dead! We were waiting for you to come heal him, but you are too late. You could have helped him if you had come sooner."

Martha cried.

Mary cried.

Jesus cried too.

Everyone watching said, "Jesus must have loved his friend Lazarus very much."

It's a sad story. Jesus didn't come right away. Lazarus died. Everyone was sad. But the story didn't end there, **BECAUSE . . .**

Jesus is stronger than death. Jesus went to the cave where Lazarus was buried. He told the people to roll the big stone away, and in a loud voice Jesus said,

Lazarus,
COME OUT.

People who are dead can't hear.
They can't stand up.
They can't walk.

But as soon as Jesus called his name, Lazarus's eyes popped open. He jumped up and began walking to Jesus.

Jesus can bring dead people
back to life!

Are you afraid of death?

We don't need to be afraid of death, because Jesus is stronger than death. Jesus can bring dead people back to life.

STORY 40
Jesus Rides
into Jerusalem

Matthew 21:4–9
Luke 19:35–40
Zechariah 9:9–10

For three years, Jesus's friends followed him while he taught God's people. Jesus's friends saw many amazing things!

They saw Jesus turn water into wine and calm stormy seas. They saw Jesus fill nets with fish and heal sick people. They even saw Jesus bring dead people back to life!

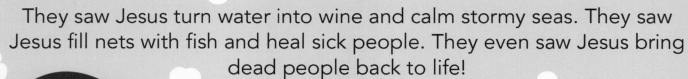

Now it was time for Jesus to go to the big city of Jerusalem. Two of his friends found a donkey for Jesus to ride. Jesus climbed up on the donkey and began riding toward Jerusalem.

His friends walked with him and sang about all the wonderful things they had seen Jesus do.

"Hooray!" they sang, "Jesus is good and powerful! Jesus truly comes from God! Jesus is a friend to children and sinners!"

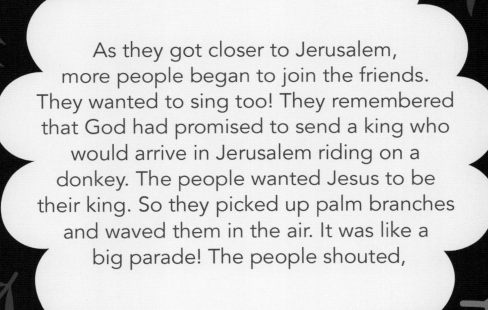

As they got closer to Jerusalem, more people began to join the friends. They wanted to sing too! They remembered that God had promised to send a king who would arrive in Jerusalem riding on a donkey. The people wanted Jesus to be their king. So they picked up palm branches and waved them in the air. It was like a big parade! The people shouted,

"Praise Jesus! He is our King!"

But some of the people did not sing. Some people did not want Jesus to be their king. The Pharisees were jealous of Jesus. They wanted the people to praise them instead.

Then Jesus told the Pharisees,
"You cannot stop the singing. If the people are quiet,
the rocks on the ground will start singing and praising me."

Why do we praise Jesus?

Jesus has done wonderful things for us. We praise him because Jesus is the King God promised.

In the big city of Jerusalem, Jesus and his friends met together in the upstairs room of a house. They sat on the floor around a low table and ate supper together.

While Jesus and his friends ate, they retold the old story about how God had freed his people from slavery in Egypt. They remembered how God had rescued them and made them into a new family.

Everyone who trusts Jesus is part of his forever family.

Jesus gave his friends a new meal called communion
to help them trust him and remember him.

Eat

Jesus took some bread and a cup of wine. He said thank you to God.
Then he broke the bread into pieces. Jesus gave the bread to his
friends and said, "This bread is broken just like my body will be broken
to pay for your sin. Eat this bread, and remember me."

Next, Jesus passed the cup to his friends so they could take a drink.

Jesus said, "This wine was poured out into a cup just like my blood will be poured out for you. Now you are a part of my forever family. Drink from this cup, and remember me."

What helps you remember your family?

We make picture albums and tell stories to help us remember our families. Everyone who trusts Jesus becomes part of his forever family. He gave us communion to help us trust and remember him.

STORY 42
Jesus Dies
for Us

Luke 22—23
1 Peter 3:18
Romans 5:8

After supper, Jesus and his friends walked to a garden to pray. Judas came too, but he didn't come to pray. Judas brought soldiers with him to take Jesus away from his friends. Judas had pretended to be Jesus's friend, but he was really Jesus's enemy.

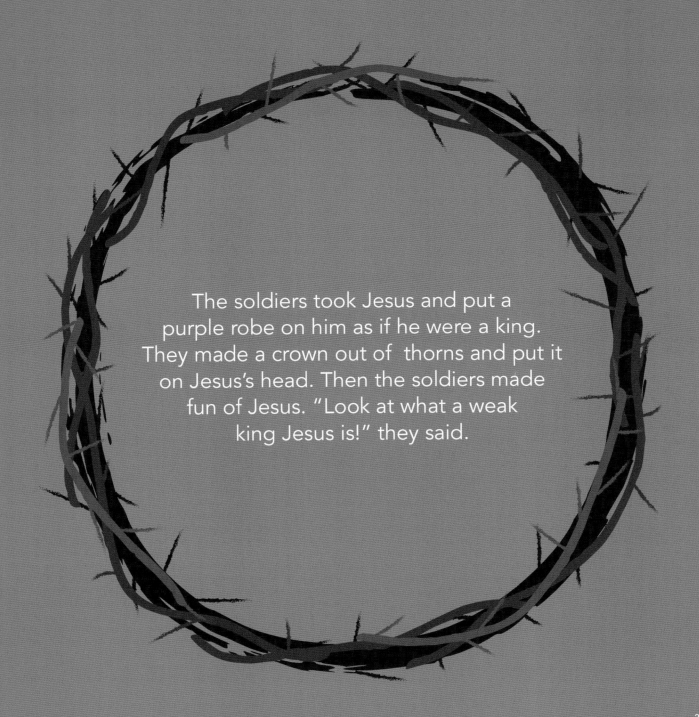

The soldiers took Jesus and put a purple robe on him as if he were a king. They made a crown out of thorns and put it on Jesus's head. Then the soldiers made fun of Jesus. "Look at what a weak king Jesus is!" they said.

Next the soldiers punched
Jesus with their fists and
hit him with whips.

They made Jesus carry a heavy
wooden cross up a big hill.

Jesus was too weak and tired to carry the cross very far.
So the soldiers grabbed a man named Simon and
told him to carry the cross for Jesus.

At the top of the hill,
the soldiers put Jesus
on the cross.

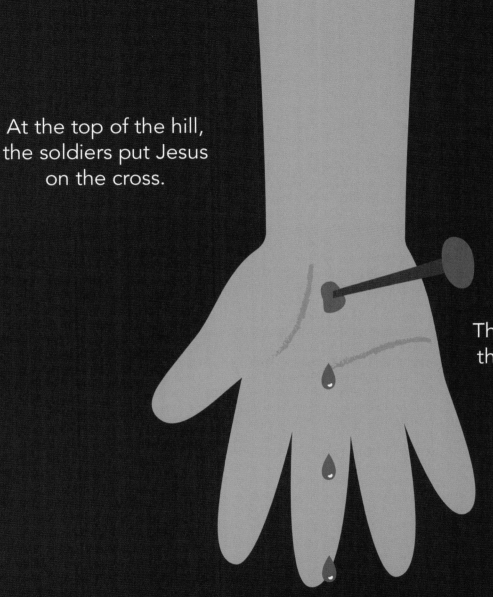

They hammered nails
through Jesus's feet
and hands,

and they left Jesus there to die.

On the cross, Jesus showed us how much he loves us. Jesus died on the cross for us even though he had never sinned or done anything wrong.

Jesus died because **WE** do wrong things.
Jesus took the punishment for **OUR** disobedience and sin.

Jesus died
instead of us.

Have you ever asked Jesus to forgive you for your sins?

Jesus died for the sins of every one of his people. When Jesus died on the cross, he took the punishment that we deserve for our sin just as he and God the Father had planned. We can be forgiven because even when we were not God's friends, Jesus died for us.

After Jesus died, his friends wrapped his body with strips of cloth. They put his body in a cave called a tomb.

Roman soldiers rolled a big stone in front of the tomb. They told guards to stand there and make sure no one tried to take Jesus's body away.

A few days passed. Then, early Sunday morning, there was an earthquake! A bright, shining angel came down from heaven. He rolled the big rock away from the front of the tomb.

The guards shook with fear.

" Ahhhh!"

Two women came by and saw that the rock was not in front of the tomb anymore. The cave was empty, and Jesus's body was missing!

The angel told the women, "Don't be afraid. Jesus is not here. Jesus has risen from the dead. Jesus is alive!"

Then the angel said, "Quickly, go and tell Jesus's friends." The women obeyed. They ran out of the garden, down the road, and into town. They found Jesus's friends and told them,

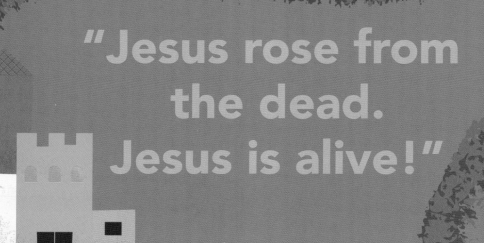

"Jesus rose from the dead. Jesus is alive!"

Peter and John were amazed. Could the women be telling the truth?

They wanted to see.
So, they ran out of town and up the road to the tomb.
When they got there, John peeked inside.
It WAS true! Jesus was not there.
Jesus is alive!

Why do we celebrate Easter?

The Sunday when Jesus rose from the dead is called Easter Sunday. Every Easter we celebrate that Jesus is more powerful than death. Jesus rose from the dead. Jesus is alive!

Two of Jesus's friends walked down a road. While they walked, a man joined them and started walking beside them.

Do you know who the man was? It was Jesus! But Jesus's friends didn't know who he was. Do you know why? Jesus hid his face from his friends. He didn't want them to recognize him right away.

Jesus's friends were talking while they walked. They were saying,

"We're so sad! Jesus was good and did amazing things, but now he is dead. We miss Jesus. We wish we could see him again!"

Jesus kept listening.
Finally, he told the friends,
"I know where you can
find Jesus.

The whole Bible
tells us about Jesus."

Jesus started teaching his friends stories from the Bible.

"Jesus is the Savior God promised to Adam and Eve.

Jesus is the wise King—even wiser than Solomon.

Jesus died for sins and then rose again on the third day!"

The three people arrived at a house. They sat down to eat. Jesus took a loaf of bread and broke it into pieces. He smiled. Suddenly his friends saw who he was. "Jesus—it's you!" they said. Jesus had been with them the whole time.

Where can we find Jesus?

We find Jesus in the whole Bible. Every story is about Jesus. Everyone who trusts in Jesus will find him and be saved.

STORY 45
King Jesus Goes
Up to Heaven

Matthew 28:18–20
Luke 24:36–52
Acts 1:1–11

When Jesus rose from the dead, he defeated

sin   **and sadness**   **and death**

and everything that is a part of our broken world.

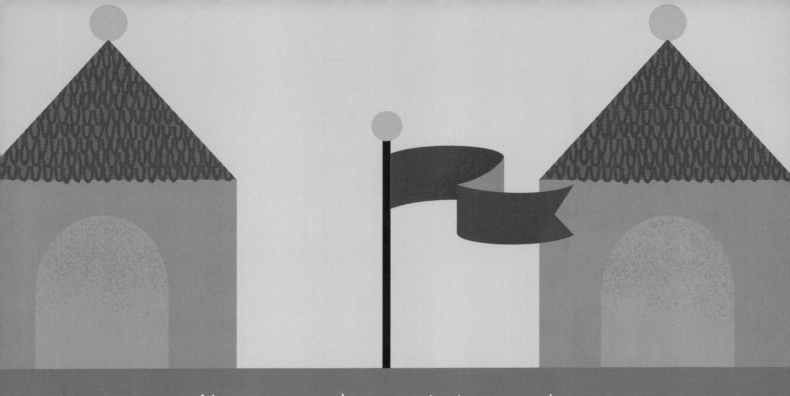

Now anyone who trusts in Jesus can be
part of a new kingdom, where Jesus is King.

267

Forty days after he rose from the dead, Jesus met with his friends.

DAY
40

THURSDAY
5

TUESDAY
3

FRIDAY
6

SUNDAY
1

MONDAY
2

WEDNESDAY
4

Jesus told them, "Go and tell the whole world about my kingdom!"

Jesus promised, "I will send the Holy Spirit to help you. He will go with you to help you tell people about my love."

Jesus sends us out to share his love.

SATURDAY

7

After Jesus said this, his friends watched
as he was lifted high into a cloud.

Up, up, up!

The cloud covered Jesus
so his friends could not see him anymore.
Jesus went up to be with his Father in heaven.

Jesus's friends stood for a long time, looking up into
the cloud. They wanted to see Jesus one more time.

While the friends were still looking, two angels appeared and said,

"Why are you looking up into heaven? King Jesus is ruling there with his Father. But one day he will come back! So, go and do what he said to do."

How do we get ready for Jesus to come back?

We can tell our friends and neighbors about King Jesus. We can share his love with the whole world.

King Jesus
sent his friends to tell
the world about him.

But he also gave them a promise. Do you remember
what Jesus promised to give his friends? Jesus said,
"I will send my Holy Spirit to go with you."

The Holy Spirit is God, just like Jesus and the Father are God.

All three are one God.
We cannot see the Holy Spirit.

He does not have a body like ours. But the Holy Spirit is God, and he lives with everyone who trusts in Jesus.

Jesus's friends remembered his promise,
and they waited for the Holy Spirit.

They prayed and they waited.
Then they prayed and waited some more.

Suddenly Jesus's friends
heard a loud rushing sound.

WHOOOOSH!

They saw strange little flames of fire over each person's head.
The Holy Spirit had come!

The friends went outside to tell people about Jesus. Many people heard the good news and trusted in King Jesus.

The Holy Spirit helped thousands of people become a part of God's new kingdom!

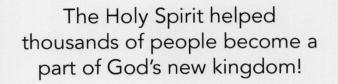

Who can help us tell people about Jesus?

If we trust in Jesus, the Holy Spirit lives with us. The Holy Spirit helps us tell others about Jesus.

The Crippled Beggar Walks!

Acts 3

Once there was a man with crippled and crooked legs.

His legs were so weak that he couldn't get out of bed to go to work. He couldn't walk to visit his friends.

Every day, the man's friends carried him to the temple in Jerusalem so he could sit by the gate and ask people for money.

People who saw the man felt sorry for him.
Sometimes they gave him money.

The man could use
the money to buy
food or clothes,
but money couldn't
fix his crooked legs.

One day,
Peter and John went to
pray at the temple.

They saw the man with crooked legs sitting by the gate. "Will you help me?" the man asked Peter and John. "Will you give me some money for food?"

Peter and John felt sorry for the man with crooked legs. But Peter said, "We don't have any money. We don't have silver or gold. But . . .

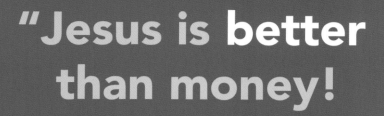

"Jesus is better than money!

Jesus can give you something money can't give you."

Then Peter told the man, **"Get up and walk!"**

Peter grabbed the man's hand and helped him stand up. Right away, the man's legs were strong and healthy. His legs weren't crooked at all!

The man jumped up and walked around, saying, "Praise Jesus! He fixed my legs. He made me well."

What can fix a broken world?

Some people think having enough money to buy food or clothes is all we need. But only King Jesus can fix our broken world. Jesus is better than money. Jesus is better than anything else!

Philip lived in Jerusalem. He helped God's people there. Sometimes Philip helped by taking food to people who had nothing to eat. Sometimes Philip helped by teaching the Bible.

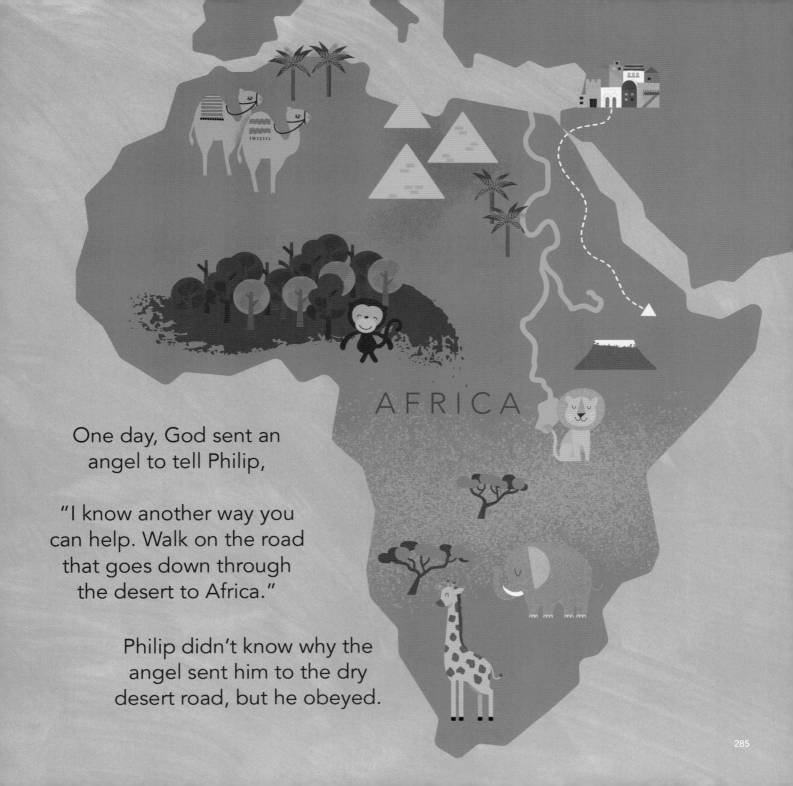

One day, God sent an angel to tell Philip,

"I know another way you can help. Walk on the road that goes down through the desert to Africa."

Philip didn't know why the angel sent him to the dry desert road, but he obeyed.

Philip looked down the road. He saw a chariot pulled by two horses.

He saw an important man sitting in the chariot. The man worked for the queen of Ethiopia. He was reading a Bible scroll, but he was confused.

Philip ran up to the chariot. He asked the man, "Can I help you?"

The official said, "Can you explain what I'm reading?"

Philip said, "Yes! I help people understand God's Word." So, beginning with the Bible scroll, Philip explained to him all about Jesus.

God sends teachers to help us **understand** his Word.

Who can help us understand God's Word?

Sometimes we don't understand, but Jesus knows how to help us. He gives us moms and dads and pastors and Sunday school teachers to help us learn about Jesus.

Do you know what happened? The Ethiopian man trusted in Jesus! Because he trusted Jesus, he stopped the chariot near some water, and Philip baptized him.

STORY 49
Saul Is Knocked
to the Ground

Acts 8:1–3; 9:1–31;
22:3–16; 26:9–18
Romans 5:6–11

Saul was an angry Pharisee.

He did not trust Jesus.
Saul hated Jesus.
And he hated Jesus's friends.

Saul went from house to house in Jerusalem looking for Jesus's friends. He dragged them out of their homes, and he locked them up in jail.

One day, Saul met with other people who hated Jesus. Saul said, "Let's travel to the city of Damascus. We'll find more of Jesus's friends there, and we'll put them in jail too!"

Could anyone stop Saul from being angry? Could anyone stop Saul from hating Jesus and Jesus's friends?

Yes!

God can change hearts.

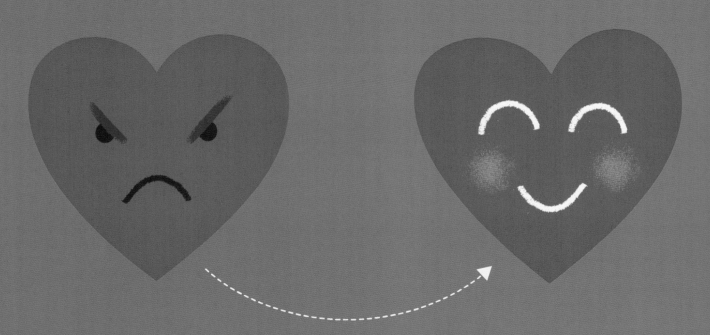

God makes enemies into friends.

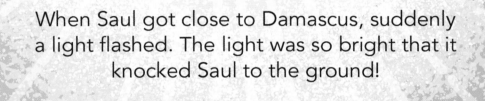

When Saul got close to Damascus, suddenly a light flashed. The light was so bright that it knocked Saul to the ground!

Saul heard a voice calling him from the light, "Saul!" The voice said, "Saul, why are you hurting my friends?" It was Jesus's voice! Jesus told Saul to go into Damascus and wait. Jesus would send someone to tell Saul what to do.

Saul obeyed Jesus. He went to Damascus. A man named Ananias came to him. Ananias loved Jesus.

Saul said, "I'm sorry. I was wrong to hate Jesus's friends. I met Jesus, and now I love Jesus, too."

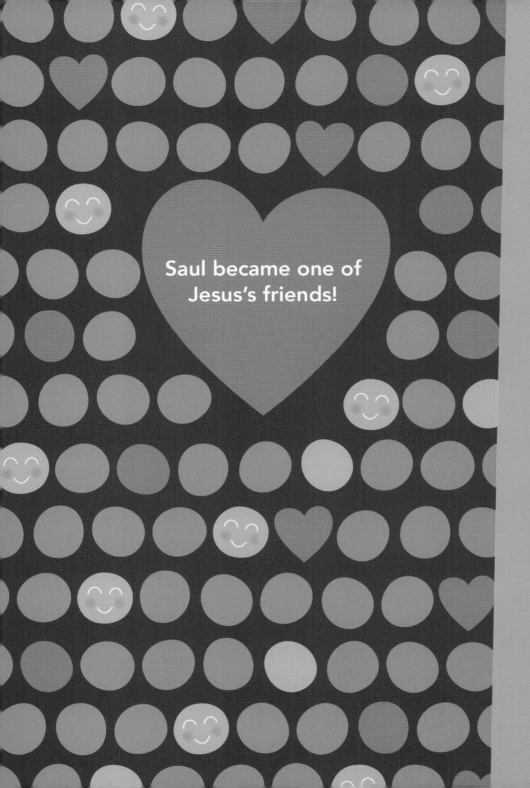

Saul became one of Jesus's friends!

Can God change sinners?

Yes! God loved Saul. God turned Saul's anger into love. God changes enemies into friends.

Peter and Cornelius were VERY different.

Peter was from Israel.
Cornelius was from Rome.

Peter wore a tunic
and a robe.
Cornelius wore a
fancy toga.
Peter ate fish, lamb,
and vegetables.
Cornelius ate
lasagna with pork
and shrimp.

296

God loves **ALL** kinds of people.

Peter was proud to be different. He was a part of God's special people. That means that Peter was very careful to eat only what God said his special people should eat. Peter NEVER disobeyed God's food rules until . . .

One day Peter sat on a balcony looking at the sea. Suddenly, he saw a blanket floating down from the sky. There were all kinds of animals on the blanket—rabbits and lions and camels and pigs.

They were all animals that Peter was not allowed to eat! But then God said something surprising. God told Peter that he could eat all the animals on the blanket.

Peter was shocked.
God was changing the food rules! God said to Peter, "I want you to show everyone that I love ALL kinds of people, no matter what kind of food they eat."

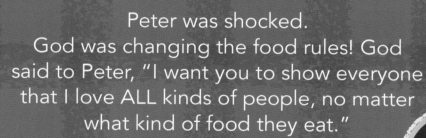

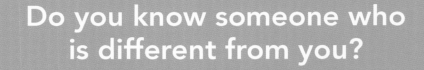

Do you know someone who is different from you?

Our friends might wear different clothes or eat different food or even speak a different language. But we can love our friends, because God loves ALL kinds of people. And God loves you too!

Next, Peter heard a knock at the door. Some people invited Peter to Cornelius's house. So, Peter went to see Cornelius and they talked about Jesus together. Peter and Cornelius prayed together, and they even **ATE** together.

Maybe they had lasagna!

More and more people learned about Jesus. They heard how Jesus died on the cross for their sins. They heard how Jesus rose from the dead and appeared to his friends. They heard how Jesus sent the Holy Spirit. Many of these people trusted Jesus.

The people who trusted Jesus met together every week.

They sang songs to God.
They studied the Bible together.
They gave money to help others.
They were the new church!

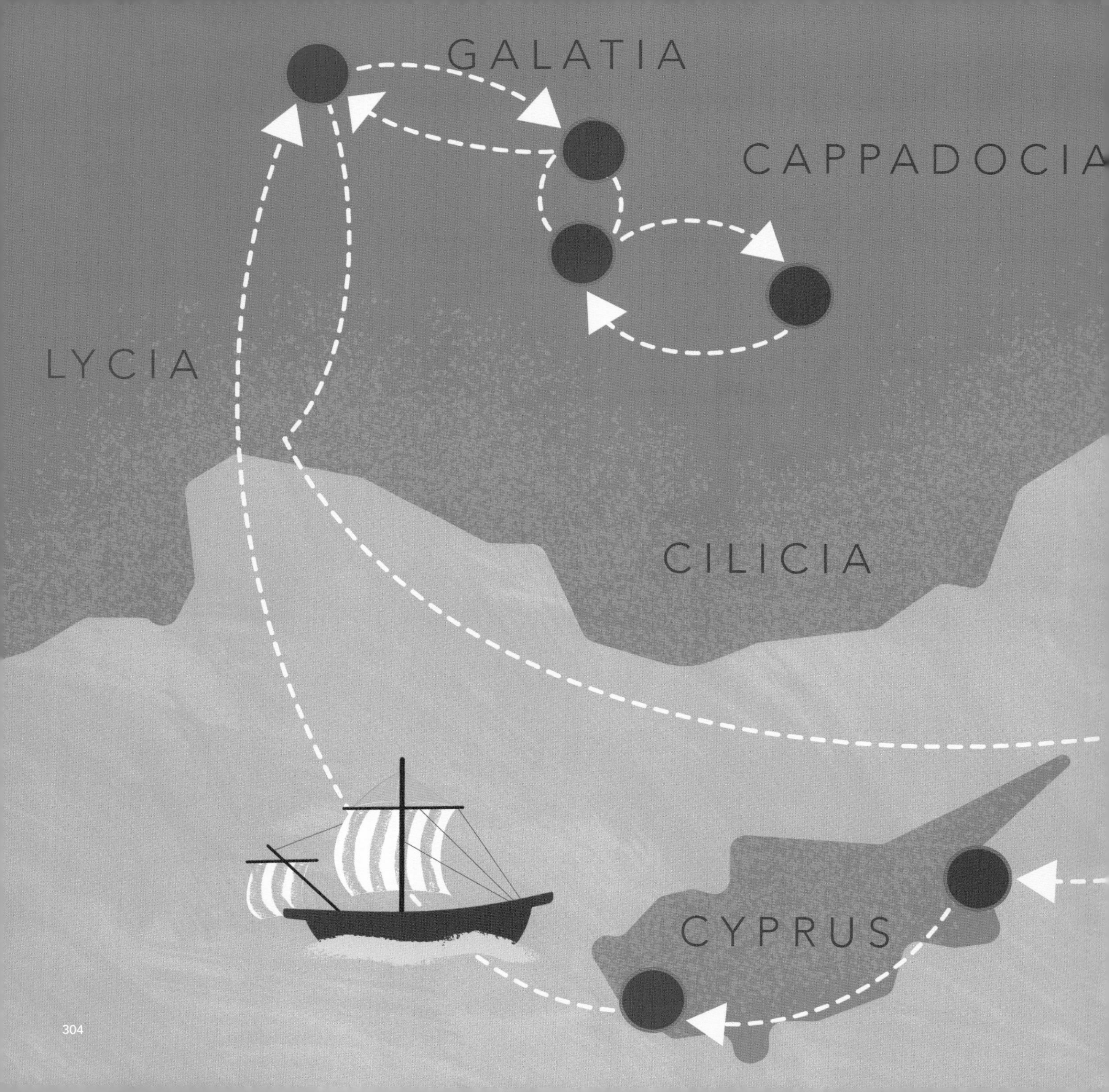

GALATIA

CAPPADOCIA

LYCIA

CILICIA

CYPRUS

One day God told the church to send Paul (who used to be called Saul) and his friend Barnabas to tell more people about Jesus. The church prayed for Paul and Barnabas and then sent them to faraway places where people had never heard of Jesus.

Paul and Barnabas traveled all over the world telling people about Jesus. They told people to stop worshiping pretend gods and trust in Jesus instead.

SYRIA

FINISH

START

Sometimes when Paul taught about Jesus, it made people angry. They threw rocks at Paul and beat him with sticks. Sometimes they put Paul in jail.

Did this make Paul angry or sad? **No!**

No matter where he was—even in jail—Paul told everyone he met about Jesus. He told the jailers and guards and other prisoners about Jesus. He even told judges and kings at court about Jesus.

He knew that God's plan was to save people from every part of the world.

Nothing can stop God's plan to save people!

Is telling people about Jesus easy?

No, sometimes telling people about Jesus is difficult and scary. But we can be brave even when we are afraid, because the Holy Spirit promises to help us. Nothing can stop God's plan to save people.

Jesus's friend John had a dream. In his dream, John saw a great throne in heaven. God sat on the throne with a bright rainbow all around him.

308

Some of God's people stood with mighty angels around the throne. They all sang, "Our mighty God is King! God made everything!"

In God's right hand, he held an old book. God's book tells everything about the world—what had happened in the past and what will happen in the future. God wrote all these things down. Then he closed the book and sealed it shut with seven seals.

One of the angels asked, "Who is good enough to break the seals and open God's book?" The angels looked and looked, but no one was good enough. So, John began to cry. He wanted to read the book!

Then someone said,
"Don't cry. Jesus can open the book! He is good enough!"

Then Jesus came and broke the seals. He opened
God's book and started to read the story to John.

The book says that God's enemy, that old snake Satan, will come like a **dragon**.

He will try to hurt God's people.
There will be terrible days.
There will be wars
and earthquakes.

Satan will hurt God's people, but
he won't be able to destroy them.

Then, on the last day,

Jesus will come back.

Jesus will come like a hero, riding on a white horse. Jesus will defeat Satan. Then Jesus will live with his people forever! God will keep all his promises.

Will God's people finally be rescued?

Yes! When Jesus comes back, he will fix our broken world. There will be no more sin or sickness. There will be no more crying or pain. Come back, Jesus! Come back quickly!

For Rachael, Lucy, and Elisabeth

Acknowledgments

Jared: I'm so grateful for Marty Machowski's trust in me as a young pastor and writer. Thank you for taking a chance on me. Thanks to Brittany Jennings, Tessa Janes, Annie Kratzsch, and Rachel Davila for all your hard work in the early stages of this book. You helped to shape what this book has become. A big thanks for the team at New Growth Press for shepherding this project from beginning to end—especially Barbara Juliani, tireless editor Nancy Winter, Gretchen Logterman, and Cheryl White. Thank you to the leadership of Sojourn Community Church for allowing me the freedom to write. Thank you to Dr. Iain Duguid for your careful theological review. Thank you to Trish Mahoney for sharing your talents as an illustrator. It has been a joy to partner with you. Finally, the biggest thanks goes to my wife Megan. She read every story, made copy edits, and gave incredibly helpful feedback. Her hand shaped every page. Only God sees all the little sacrifices you make to help me and serve our family. Thank you. I can truly say of all these amazing people, "they are the glorious ones in whom is all my delight" (Psalm 16:3). *Soli Deo Gloria.*

Trish: Thank you to the fabulous team at New Growth Press: Karen, Barbara, Nancy, Gretchen, and Cheryl, for giving me the opportunity to take on such a huge responsibility and for giving me so much creative freedom in the process— you've been a dream to work with. Jared Kennedy, thank you for partnering with me and for trusting me with your words. To my kids, Alden and Tula, thank you for your patience as I worked on this for the past year, and for your (sometimes brutal) honesty in seeing each illustration through the eyes of a child. Most of all, thanks to my husband and partner, Patrick. It was only possible to complete this book with your support and encouragement.